Goose River Anthology, 2016

Edited by

Deborah J. Benner

Goose River Press
Waldoboro, Maine

Library of Congress Card Number: 2016914354

ISBN: 978-1-59713-171-1

First Printing, 2016

Cover photo by Kasey M. Benner

Published by
Goose River Press
3400 Friendship Road
Waldoboro ME 04572
e-mail: gooseriverpress@roadrunner.com
www.gooseriverpress.com

Authors Included

Authors Included

In Memory of

Anne W. Hammond

&

Bill Tucker

Goose River Anthology, 2016

the late Bill Tucker
Aurora, OH

Why Don't People Like Me?

When I was in the ninth grade, I had some strange thing wrong with me that lasted for about two months, practically all summer. I mean, I was sick with something and the doctor didn't really know what it was, although he acted like he did. My mother always said, now that she had a chance to look back on it, that she thinks it must have been polio. She's completely wrong about that. It wasn't anything like polio, but she keeps saying it anyhow. She wished it was, I suppose, and so do I because I'd be immune now. That's not important, though. This isn't going to be about me having polio.

The main thing is that I had this long spell of sickness and I had to stay in bed for over two months. Whatever it was must have just worn itself out because nothing the doctor did seemed to have had anything to do with my getting well. The point is that I was so weak when Momma finally let me get up—that was after I had gone three days without fever—I could hardly walk. I was so skinny I had trouble keeping my pants on. It's funny what you remember, but I remember the pants I put on when I got up that first time, a kind of washed out holey-knee blue denim.

Momma helped me around the house and made me sit out in the sun in the front yard. The kids would come by, especially Ernest Sanders, and keep me company. It was a whole lot better than being in bed.

Ernest was a year older than me and about my best friend. He put in a lot of time just sitting around with me when he could have been out at the ball park or the river. I really appreciated it.

For some reason I just couldn't seem to get over whatever that thing was I had. I don't mean to say I still had it, but I just wasn't especially healthy even a couple of years after

the late Bill Tucker
Aurora, OH

that. When I started going to high school I only weighed about a hundred and I was as tall as I am now, maybe an inch shorter. All that time, since I had been sick, Momma kept worrying about me and trying to fatten me up with anything that was supposed to do it. The thing that did the most good was malted milk. She used to buy the malt ready mixed with chocolate and shake me up a big glass every night. It was pretty grainy and didn't taste much like what you get at the ice cream shop, but after a while I got to where I really liked the stuff; I still drink it almost every night. Of course I shake it up myself now. About five pounds was all I gained in two years and Momma still says that the only thing that kept me alive was that malted milk.

Ernest first put the idea in my head about going out for football. When he said he thought I ought to, said it would build me up, I really gave him the horse-laugh. I could see myself out there with all those big boys. Some of them were old enough to vote and must have weighted two hundred. Man, they would kill me. But he explained that I would just be fooling around with the scrubs, taking exercise mostly.

I had to admit that Ernest hadn't been hurt any by going out. He had been out a year and you could really tell the difference in him. He's always been shorter than me but he must have weighed a hundred and fifty. This year he said Coach was going to let him scrimmage and try out for a spot on the traveling B-team. The B-team has a schedule just like the varsity.

I finally wound up going out for the team. I got to thinking about it and I didn't enjoy looking like a scarecrow. About that time I was getting pretty worked up about girls, and they wouldn't give me the time of day. I was so scrawny I guess they thought they might hurt me or something. Anyway, I talked with Dad about it and he really liked the idea. It must have worried him, though, because he had a long talk with Coach about it. The way Coach put it was that the exercise would be good for me. I could tell by the way

the late Bill Tucker
Aurora, OH

Dad went over what they had said that Coach was pretty unenthusiastic about the whole idea. I can't blame him; Coach knew what I looked like and he couldn't see much football material. That was okay with me, though. I wasn't really interested in football anyway. It would help if the girls just knew I was going out.

Dad had to get kind of tough to make my momma understand. Well, not exactly understand, I don't think she ever has understood why it was so important for me to go out. She still thought I was a hospital case, I guess. But I believe my dad was always a little ashamed of me for being such a dried up little fart. Finally he had to lay down the law. When I think about it now, I see that he must have been pretty determined, after he once got the idea. I'm surprised it hadn't occurred to him before I mentioned it. He's always been such an active guy. You should see the muscles he's still got in his arms. Most guys at forty-five or fifty are pretty flabby, but his stomach is as flat as mine is. Lots of times he goes to the river with us and there's only about two other guys, besides him, that will dive off the top of Quin's bridge. It's about forty feet.

The first year there really isn't anything to tell about, except the weight I gained. Coach even lets the scrubs come out and knock each other around during spring practice. So I was out running around and taking exercises the whole year. By the time school was out in May I weighed one forty-two. All the time I was putting that weight on I could see my dad getting all swelled up about it. I could tell what he had in his mind and it worried me because I still didn't really go for football all that much. The best thing about it was the way my momma stopped treating me like a sick little kid. As soon as the grass started to grow she put me to mowing it and had me lifting things she should have used a horse for. She still bucked a little when Dad kept talking about me going out for B-team the next year but I could see that nothing she could say, or me either for that matter, was going to

the late Bill Tucker
Aurora, OH

change his mind about me being a football player.

Another thing was that the girls didn't look at me like I was a freak any more. Most of them didn't look at me at all; girls don't look at freshmen to amount to anything. But I could tell there was a difference. As a matter of fact there were a couple of girls in my own class that taught me how to dance that summer, and I was kissing both of them a lot before school started, and I was a sophomore.

Old Ernest worried that summer about still being one-fifty and by the time we both showed up for B-team in the fall I weighted as much as he did. He kept saying he never was going to get any bigger, and, the way it worked out, he didn't. He stayed the same size until he graduated. Anyway, he was a junior and worried a lot about whether he was going to make the varsity trips even before we started practice. The way Coach works the varsity and B-teams is that there are only about twelve or thirteen guys on the varsity that don't play on the B-team. The rest of the guys that dress out for the varsity games do. I don't know what Ernest was worrying about because he was going to be starting right half-back on the B-team and he knew it. That assured him of making the varsity trips, but I didn't know it at the time.

The way the guys on the varsity do is pick out some guy like me who has just graduated from the scrubs for a year of misery. They knock you around a lot when you play on a dummy team for them to run signals. And they really give you a poke in the face or a stiff arm if you scrimmage against them. Things like that. The guy that picked me out was a guard that probably was the greatest punter we ever had. When it came time to punt he always dropped out of the line to do it. He only weighed about fifteen pounds more than I did but he easily worked me over. The thing he did the most was check block in the line and come down on me when I was playing defensive left half-back. He would jump up in the air right in front of me and then twist over and wrap all around me. He never missed no matter what I did.

the late Bill Tucker
Aurora, OH

Sometimes when we were just running signals he would come at me like he was really going to throw a block and then he would just jump up in a kind of jack-knife and stick his tail in my chest. It knocked me down every time and he got a big kick out of it. In a way it was kind of funny to me too. It seemed like I was either on the ground or just getting up all the time. Every once in a while when the guard would knock me down I'd look over at Coach and he'd be grinning and shaking his head. I guess he was thinking he never was going to make a football player out of me.

One thing that surprised me was that there were a couple of guys working on Ernest, an end and a tackle, both big guys. Coach even let him run a few plays with the varsity every now and then, but these guys were still working on him, especially when we scrimmaged. Whenever he was their blocking assignment, they really let him have it. Boy, there was no place for him to hide out there. But then he didn't act like he wanted to. No matter what they did he never said a word, but he didn't smile either. He was in there trying all the time, like everything depended on them not getting him, like making the tackle was the most important thing in his life. When they let the second string run offense he was the same way. When he carried the ball he'd tear into those big guys with his head down just as if they had been blocked out of the way like they were supposed to be. I almost had to close my eyes every time he did that. I couldn't see how he could keep getting up, the way they hit him.

It took me a long time but I began to see what was wrong. Maybe you could say it was Ernest not ever smiling about the way they worked on him. But I guess it was just that he tried too hard. Don't get me wrong; I try hard and so do all the other guys. We don't get out of the way of a tough tackle or slow up when we see we're about to get hit, but there's a difference. The way Ernest went about it, it was a pretty grim business; he just tried too hard. It seemed like he was shouting at these big guys: "I'll show ya." I didn't see what

the late Bill Tucker
Aurora, OH

he was trying to prove. He didn't have to prove anything.

Up until that year I guess I just didn't know much about Ernest. He was my best friend and I really didn't know anything at all about him. One thing I found out is that he was about the smartest guy in school. One of the English teachers, who is a cousin of mine, said he had an almost photographic memory. She came over to the house one night and got to talking about some of the things he had done in her class. It was really amazing, the things he could remember. But old Ernest wasn't satisfied with getting good grades without half trying. He knocked himself out with the books, too. It seemed like he couldn't stand anybody else knowing something he didn't know. I guess I'm pretty ignorant when it comes to comparing myself with Ernest, but I get along okay. That is, my grades were nothing to be ashamed of. I'm three, maybe four, from the top of my class. The ones ahead of me are girls, maybe one guy. But there's a difference in the way I feel about it, I guess. It would sure take all the fun out of school if I worried about not being first. Maybe I couldn't be and knew it and that's why I don't really stay with the books.

Anyway, that's beside the point I was making about Ernest. I keep thinking he's trying too hard and taking all the fun out of it. He seems like the kind of guy that sits in front of the radio and shouts out the answers before the guy on the quiz program gets it.

For some reason things really started to break right for me. I made the B-team backfield and Coach let me dress out for the home varsity games that year. I even got to play for a few minutes in all but one game. We had a good season, lost only one, and that was the one where I didn't get to play. I started making out with the girls a little, too. My dad was pretty good about letting me use the car and I made all the dances. I learned to jitterbug and by the time football season was over I was in pretty solid with the girls even a year older, the ones in Ernest's class. That was probably because I started going pretty steady with this girl that moved into

the late Bill Tucker
Aurora, OH

town in the middle of the Fall semester. She was a year ahead of me, a junior and as good looking as any of the girls in school. All the guys, even the seniors, gave her the big rush. I couldn't believe it when she kept going out with me. But I kind of got in with the older crowd and didn't have much to do with the sophomores after that. I even dated some of the other junior girls. It seemed like my class had an unusually large bunch of ugly girls.

Then the next season, that was the last year, Ernest and I were starting varsity. Like I said, everything broke right for me. I wouldn't have been first string quarterback if it hadn't been for Earl going into the Army. When we started practice things seemed to be entirely different with Ernest. He really seemed to be enjoying not taking it so seriously. The big guys seemed like they had let up. The tackle that had worked on him, Jesse Harrell, was still on the team, but he didn't do anything you could really notice. Jesse is a funny guy anyway. He is big and rawboned and pretty much of a loner. Most of the time you had the feeling he didn't even know you were alive.

But when it got close to our first game, Ernest started getting just like he had been before—got this grim determined way about him. And I could notice a difference in the team, not just Jess, but all the rest of the guys. It was even making me nervous.

It took a couple of games for me to see what was happening, but when I finally realized what these guys in our line were doing, I just didn't want to believe it They were letting the other team's guys in on Ernest. Oh, they weren't obvious about it and it only happened when it didn't make any difference, like the last couple of plays before the half when we didn't have a chance to score or when we were so far ahead it didn't make any difference. But they would slide off their blocks and let the guards and tackles in, or they'd just miss a red-dogging end and Ernest would get a helmet in the face. He took some pretty rough stuff and I think he knew it before

the late Bill Tucker
Aurora, OH

I did. You've got to hand it to him; he never said a word.

I suppose Ernest wanted to be senior class president more than he wanted to be first-string varsity. In a lot of little ways you could tell he was wanting to be nominated when the time came and it worked out that he was. This girl, Florence Severns, nominated him. The senior class elections are a pretty big production. After you're nominated you have three days to work up your votes before the ballots are cast. I knew it was hard for old Ernest, but he went around talking it up, dead serious about it like he was about everything else.

I remember the night before the election we were walking around down town and Ernest was buttonholing every senior he saw for votes. He had already asked everybody at least once at school, but he was still trying. To tell the truth, I was getting kind of tired about it. There was a group of guys, about four or five, loafing around by the gas company office. They must have just come down from the skating rink on the second floor and didn't want to go home. I didn't see Jesse Harrell until we had walked up to them and I was hoping Ernest wasn't going to ask him for a vote. But two other guys were seniors and he asked them all. You'd have to know Ernest to know just how it was he asked them. It was like they would be pretty stupid if they didn't vote for him. I think he sounded like that because it was so important to him.

Before anybody could say anything Jesse came over and leaned down into Ernest's face.

"You're a silly shit, Sanders," he said quietly, but he wasn't joking. Man, he wasn't joking.

There wasn't anything Ernest could do. Jesse would have wiped up the sidewalk with him if he'd done anything. And I'd have had to get into it too, one way or another. Right then I didn't want anything to do with Jesse Harrell.

I took Ernest by the arm and pulled him around. He hadn't said anything and still didn't while I was dragging him off down the street. For two or three blocks I could feel him working up to whatever it was he was going to say. Brother,

the late Bill Tucker
Aurora, OH

was I dreading it! But the longer he waited the more I wished he would go on and say it and get it over with.

As we were about to turn into the street that goes in front of my house, he just didn't turn but walked over to the curb and sat down under the street light. There wasn't anything for me to do but go over and sit down with him and wait.

"Why don't people like me, Red?"

Now what the hell can you say to a question like that? For crying out loud!

Old Ernest is in the Navy now. He didn't win the election, and I guess things in general just didn't go very well for him the rest of the year. This girl he wanted more than being football varsity or senior-class president just strung him along. She broke dates with him to go out with damn near anybody—soldiers she'd just met, for instance.

I've thought about it and I still can't say for sure. Why people didn't like Ernest much, I mean. I liked him a hell of a lot.

***

Robert Hodum
Sound Beach, NY

Seen from Here

A bluff settles in at dusk,
Receding under shadows that pull over
Its well-worn tracks and brush,
Somewhere in the blue darkness of that edge
Lies a threshold gone missing,
As twilight blurs certainty

Jennifer Lunden
Portland, ME

In February: After a Complaint to My Acupuncturist Before Getting on Her Table

There's not even reason for hope till April.
The robins will come, but they will be the Canadian robins,
Which come in February, and not the American ones, which
       come in spring.
I've heard rumors from points south that people have heard
       birds singing,
That snowmen are listing in the thaw.

But another polar vortex is on its way.

T.S. Eliot said April is the cruelest month,
But he had not lived in Maine in February.
Don't the lilacs bloom in April?
Don't the tulips burst through the dirt?
Or is that May?

I know that in the shade of our yard the snow lingers late.
But I remember the crocuses and the tulips and the white
       daffodils.
And I remember the snowdrops because they come first.
And of course the forsythia, its garish yellow
Forgiven because it is the first color of the season.

The *Farmers' Almanac* predicted this brutal cold, these
       heaps of snow.
But every year we forget what winter means
When the first snow falls in puffy flakes
And we put our hands to our cheeks and watch in wonder.
"It's snowing!" we say, like children, forgetting, for a moment,
       the shoveling,

(continued)

**Jennifer Lunden
Portland, ME**

The cars that won't start, the slipping on sidewalks.
We remember the snow forts and snow pants and snowball
      fights.
We remember tromping through the snow, the creaking of
      the snow.
We remember the hush of the city after a freshly fallen snow.
We remember, and then we forget.

***

**Sally Belenardo
Branford, CT**

Once, Passing Their Garden

Their bungalow nestles under
the weeping cherry tree that shades ferns
and bleeding hearts. Wisteria cascades
on trellises. Moonflowers rise among
morning glory vines; the angel trumpets
proclaim their divine scent to passersby.
From doorstep to street, last frost to first,
beds of crocuses, narcissus, hyacinths
become irises, poppies, peonies, before
roses and lilies precede chrysanthemums,
sunflowers, and prize-winning dahlias
they enter in fairs.

Of a heavenly summer morning,
amidst the profusion of their Eden,
the couple conversed unnoticed, until
the man hissed a vile, withering tirade
at the woman, proving every garden
has a snake.

Goose River Anthology, 2016//11

Roselyn Stewart
Brookfield, WI

Autumn's Orchard

God's hand blesses
the peaceful orchard.
We wade shin deep
through fallen leaves.
Crushed beneath our
feet they give off
an aromatic bouquet.
The sun warms us as it
peers through gray skies.
We pick the last
stubborn apples
that cling to the trees.
Golden leaves swirl
about us.
Red apples peek through
rusty debris.
Geese forage for fallen
Treats.
A cold wind foretells
Winter.

Patti Rutka
Saco, ME

We Are Stardust

My father had been dying for some months. His mind, scuttled by advanced Alzheimer's, had more left to it than his starved body. Today or tomorrow would be the day, his last day, hospice assured me over the phone after a week of vigil. So, thirteen hundred miles distant, wheeling above an expansive early green spring, I flew from Maine to the compressed snows of a Wisconsin clinging to winter. Perhaps I could lay hold to something no child should have to touch upon—the moment at which a parent dies.

My father lived through that night I arrived late on the plane. I sat with him, the child in me frightened, and touched his cool, purple-mottled feet. I tried to understand why he still clutched life. "Maybe if we brought my mother into the room he would be able to let go," the adult in me told the hospice nurse, aching for his release, for him, for me, for our family.

My mother, at 108 pounds down from 160 in her 81st year, slept twenty hours out of twenty-four. Her doctor, fortified by his shin-length white coat and stethoscope around his neck, Oz behind the curtain, had been unable to explain to the three of us girls why she slept so much. In truth, my mother's sleeping was the greater mystery than my father's decline, but at least we understood why my father's malady rendered him unable to eat.

When I had last visited him, Wisconsin's maple leaves were shifting burnt orange, umber, twisting off their stems, sifting to dry ground on October winds. Inside his assisted living cocoon my father had been incapable of maneuvering his spoon. He'd picked up the utensil, remembering from some long-trodden neural path that it was the means with which to carry food to his mouth, but the spoon skewed off to one side of his face. Creamed corn smeared his bony cheek

Patti Rutka
Saco, ME

and plopped in his lap. So he gave up on the spoon and shuttled his fingers to his mouth, gumming them as if he could take in both nutrition and implement at once. Instead, I fed him.

Yet I lived in Maine and could not feed him every day. The home's attendants catered to him when they could, but he had signed living will directions for no feeding tubes. Come March, he was as shriveled as the fall leaves.

Now in the still room Tommy Dorsey's "Star Dust" crooned from a CD I'd burned. Music my parents had cut a rug to floated over the blanketed bodies of my parents. My mother, tiny and white-haired, curled up and asleep in a recliner like the succession of cats she'd had over the years. My father, breathing peacefully in bed with morphine, his air-hungry skeleton-mouth finally closed.

I padded around his bed, my fingers adjusting the white cotton blanket covering my daddy's emaciated shins, his knobby-jointed knees, my hands coming to rest on his feet. In my childhood he'd hummed with contentment when I'd rubbed his feet. He'd tolerated the pink plastic curlers I rolled up in his hair as he lay across our orange velour footstool after dinner, letting me play "beauty parlor" when I was six. My daddy. My daddy, who danced me on his buffed leather shoes and took me to see *Herbie the Lovebug* one weekend. My father. My rigid Navy father, who argued with me over politics in my teen years across the dinner table, scowling his disapproval of my liberal tendencies. My dad, who drank oatmeal stout with me in a Scottish pub during my graduate studies.

His feet felt even cooler now, no longer purple, but yellow. "Anchors Aweigh" played on the CD.

Then in a single movement his frail body urged upward. His boney head and open mouth sought air, once, twice, a deep chortling scrabble. With my hands on his feet his body settled, his life-lights twitching out. His chest did not rise again.

Patti Rutka
Saco, ME

I wailed on the keen air, as if my cry could press another inhalation upon him, as if I could pin my father's spirit to his bones. But his spirit, unlike his feet, was not something I could lay hands on.

My cry woke my mother, her eyes sleep-befuddled. "He's gone," I cried, helpless. Her chin puckered and one tear ran out of a blind blue-grey eye. "He was a good man," she said, and her head nodded onto her chest.

Reaching across his soon-stiffening body, I covered his cold feet with the white white blanket, squeezed them one last time, then kissed his cheek. I could have stayed in Maine. But then, I knew, every child should be so blessed to touch that moment of a parent's death.

***

Toni Ortner
Putney, VT

In the Still Night Air

In the still night air
a sudden gust of wind
whips the branches bare
tears the green leaves to tatters.

How quick the black funnel appeared
swept across the ground
tossing the horses as if they were stones
so broken bones lay in heaps with tufts of hair.

We sleep too deep.
There is a sound in silence we cannot hear.

Margaret Yocom
Farmington, ME

Swing

For Grandfather Isaac Newton Yocom (1885–1978)
of Longview Farm, Douglassville, PA

The swing, we'd beg him,
pulling him to the towering catalpa,
the high bank,
please, the swing—
the swirl of it, the flight,
to leave,
to rip loose
from daffodils and green lawn
hand-laid stone walls
jersey cows, their mouths filled with clover
hollyhocks by the gate
the lane past the chicken coops
the beehives,
up into the tree's top leaves
into summer's impossibly blue sky,
the reach of it—
each falling back was only a way
to fly higher then,
always knowing his arms were there,
the constant knotted ropes.

Steve Troyanovich
Florence, NJ

the boundary of being
for Mohammed Khair-Eddine

at the edge of ruins
winds sing of shattered
children...forsaken
memories populate
angry stars

quivering a lost rose
seeks answers to the
beckoning shadows
of phosphorescent butterflies
born to cold exiles in
forbidden suns...

dismantling the deserted asylum
a caged poet ponders
the sacramental relevance
of solitary words...
visages unearthed
cling to howling guises
ancient vocabularies
swallow up the dawn

...there is only clarity
in darkness

Peggy Trojan
Brule, WI

In the Attic

for Kelley

We cleaned out the attic
at your folks, decades after
your untimely death.
Found the box of Barbies
and all their clothes:
coats and dresses
and the bridal gown.
You had packed them
with dreams
of moving on to your own
fairy tales.

They smelled musty.
In an attempt to preserve
what you chose to save,
I washed and ironed them today,
marveling at the tiny sleeves,
the little turned collars.
Then, packed them up again,
carefully, with some
old dreams of my own.

Talking Stick 2015
Editor's Choice

Barbara Winslow
Norridgewock, ME

He Wants to Walk

He wants to walk...
Out to the barn on a clear dark winter morning,
Lean his head against the warm side of the cow,
Smell the pungent warmth of the hay,
Watch the frothy milk as it pings into the pail...

He wants to walk
Across the tundra headed to the river
Watching the geese fly low
Hearing the cranes and swans talk
as they glide into
arctic summer...

He wants to walk
Into the woods behind the farm,
a rifle in hand
a deer on his mind,
his boys by his side...

He wants to walk
Without a cane
or walker
or wheel chair.

He wants to walk.

Mark D. Biehl
Hales Corners, WI

Lake Superior Trilogy

Chattel

The lake
Now restful
In the morning calm
Belies the summer evening storm
Which roared
Unexpectantly
From East-Northeast, and ravaged
With some heretofore hidden lust
The beaches
And the dunes.

Homecoming

Ghostly shapes of silver
Carried on the shoulders of
Grey glass-edged waves,
Stretch out along the
Quieting sand
To begin their
Final rest.

Green Flash

Adirondack chairs
Snuggle on the beach
Near embers of drifted wood,
Crackling.
Sun descending to complete the candle,
Sky awash with purpled orange.
Calm seas.

Emily Hess
Elizabethtown, PA

The Blame

It starts with sisal, bound in loose skeins with strips of blue plastic twine. She sits with the skeins on her lap, unwinding and unplying the long thin reeds. The sisal is blonde, each strand thin and coarse, like the long mane of a palomino mare. It's a tedious task, cutting the sisal, and she daydreams as her silver scissors slice the long fiber strands into two inch pieces that carpet the cement floor of her studio like the shorn locks of Samson. She thinks of the sisal plant, a cactus crouching in the dry Mexican soil, like a giant pineapple with its rosette of sword-shaped leaves and its squat, scaled stem. How many miles did it travel, stripped of its belly of coarse fibers, to rest in her lap? She moves her chapped fingers over the strands.

She gathers the pieces and places them in an iron pot, its heavy base a marbled patina of copper and jade, the result of corrosion and poor cleaning. She pours water over the clippings, watching as the fibers engorge and darken, floating flaccid and lax in their tepid bath. Then two scoops of soda ash, the caustic white powder settling on the water's surface like a dusting of snow. She leaves as the pot begins its gentle boil, slipping out before the decaying fibers can fill the small shed with their bitter fumes.

She makes dinner. Her husband comes home. The pasta is overdone, gummy campanili in a pool of puttanesca. Her husband says nothing, drinks three glasses of wine. She makes a cup of chamomile, watches it grow cold. He asks her to come to bed. She frowns slightly, checks the time.

Five hours on the stove and the sisal is an acrid soup, limp strands in an amber sauce. She rinses the fibers in the sink, watching the water swirl down the drain, pale as her chamomile tea, then paler, then clear. She transfers the

Emily Hess
Elizabethtown, PA

rinsed fibers to the Hollander beater and turns the wheel to the highest setting; the motor leaps to life. Tucking her chin into her cupped hand, she sits and watches as the rotor churns, spitting flecks of sisal and white foam against its glass shield.

She falls asleep like that, lulled by the white noise of the motor and the pulp sloshing against the trough's sloped walls. Her husband comes, walking barefoot across the dew-damp lawn. He hesitates before the door of the small shed that is her studio, then pushes it open. The groan of rusty hinges is inaudible over the beater's clacking motor. He touches her shoulder and she wakens, blinking eyes moist and heavy-lidded with sleep.

He says her name. He says that it's late. He asks her again to come to bed. She looks at the beater, at the slurry swirling in its ovoid trough. She looks at her husband, at the dew-damp hems of his cotton pants.

He says please. She turns off the beater; it grinds to a halt with a soft cough and the slurry rocks with residual motion before it falls still. She slips her hand into the mixture, feeling the coarse hairs tangle between her fingers as she moves them through. A few more hours and the sisal will be a fine pulp, silk-smooth and blonde again.

She follows her husband to back to the house. Their bed is cold beneath its beige duvet. She curls on her side. Her husband kisses her neck, once, over the birthmark like a blue bruise at the nape.

In the morning, her husband fills the house with the heady scent of coffee, and she breathes deeply as she dresses, pulling in lungfuls of the warm aroma as she slips on linen pants and a blouse patterned with bluebell. As she enters the kitchen, her husband looks up from his crossword and smiles, pushing a mug of coffee toward her. She hesitates a moment, watching a plume of steam curl above the rim.

Emily Hess
Elizabethtown, PA

She walks to the door and puts on her galoshes. The air is crisp and bright, the grass still damp with early morning dew. In the trough of the Hollander beater, the sisal lies meek beneath a coat of clear water. She drags her hand through the slurry, and the settled strands rise and swirl like a flock of startled birds. Maybe she will leave them long and coarse, she thinks, watching the ribbons of sisal tangle and dance, pulled by the rhythm of the water and her hands.

She takes her rubber apron from its hook on the wall and dons it. Her favorite vat still holds two inches of thin cotton pulp. She sets a deckle box over the grate and pours the mixture through, watching the cotton gather in the box like dense, matted cloud. As she's charging the vat of sisal, pouring the thickener in and mixing, testing the lazy slosh and ripple of added viscosity, her husband comes. The door's rusty hinges whistle a warning as he crosses the room, hands cradling her rejected coffee. He sets it on the table beside the basin of sisal and says "I'm going in to the office for a few hours. I thought you might want this."

She can smell the musk and spice of his aftershave. There is a fleck of shaving cream on his jaw and her hand twitches for a moment with the urge to wipe it off. She knots her fingers into a fist, willing them still.

He takes her hand, tracing his thumb over the chapped, dry skin. He brushes his lips over the hair-thin cracks that crosshatch her knuckles, where the skin is perennially abraded by water and caustic additives. In his grasp, her hand is like something small and limp and dead.

She pulls her hand free, walks to a shelf along the wall and takes the smallest mold and deckle, the fine mesh screen in its wooden frame no larger than a postcard.

He watches as she dips the mold and deckle into the vat, pulling a sheet of sisal in a smooth, forward stroke. She turns the mold and deckle and draws another sheet, jostling the frame so the fibers settle smooth and even across the wire screen as the water drains back into the bin. She lifts

Emily Hess
Elizabethtown, PA

the deckle off and couches the sheet onto a square of wet felt, rocking the edge of the mold against the board so the sheet comes free of the mesh and lies flat in the center of the cloth.

Her husband says her name, says "Do you want to get lunch? I could pick you up in a couple hours and we could try that new place." She shakes her head.

He tries again. "Okay, well, I could get takeout and we could eat here. I could get sandwiches from the deli, or that soup with the enoki that you like." She shakes her head again.

"Damn it, Anna," he says, slamming his fist down on the table. The sisal sloshes in its vat, splashing over the rim and splattering the floor with water and fine, tangled fibers. "I don't know what you want me to do. I'm trying so hard; I've told you I'm sorry. We can't live like this. You don't eat, we never talk, or kiss or make love anymore. You won't even look at me. How long has it been since you left the house? Weeks? I don't know what to do, Anna. Please. I love you. Let me help you."

She looks at him, standing there in his grey suit, one hand still fisted on the table, the tendons pulled taut across the dorsum and wrist.

He reaches for her; his fingertips just brush her cheek as she leaps back.

"Don't." She spits the word, face rumpling. She catches her breath and holds it like a child holds a moth between cupped hands, afraid it will escape.

When he speaks again, his voice is raw and soft, and he looks at the puddle of spilled sisal on the floor between them. "We lost our baby. It happens. Sometimes it just happens and there's nothing anyone can do. We have to move on. Please, Anna."

She looks at him, eyes bright with unshed tears. She takes the mold and deckle in her hands, aligns the frames, and pulls a sheet of sisal. He watches her press the sheet, then pull a second, a third, layering the paper between pieces

Emily Hess
Elizabethtown, PA

of wet felt to form the post.

As she moves back to the vat, he intercedes. He takes the mold and deckle from her and draws a sheet of sisal. She watches his hands move through the pulp, the strands of sisal that cling to his wrists and forearms, matching the fine hairs there.

She taught him how to make paper, when they were new-lyweds. She had stood behind him, arms around his waist, coaching him through the movements—the plunge, the sweep, the pull—like a kind of dance. He used to ruin the pages on purpose, just to keep her arms around him; used to turn in her arms and kiss her, mold and deckle floating abandoned in the vat. He used to sit on the table as she worked, perched beside the vat so that she sometimes splashed his files with pulp. He would steal strands of fiber or dry sheets to use as bookmarks, or to write her love let-ters. She used to love that, the way he filled the space with his laughter, the scent of his aftershave.

"Here," he said, holding out the frame to her, a perfect sheet of sisal set on the mesh. "Is this what you want?" A dull anger deadens the words. She observes the tightness in his knuckles gripping the wood, the taut muscles in his jaw, the tension that thrums through him, of anger and grief and des-peration.

"You're my wife, Anna. And I'm your husband. We get through this together, or not at all."

She turns away, fetches a new mold and deckle from the shelf, an eight-by-eight square with water-warped edges. He watches as she draws a sheet, studies the fibers' tangled matt, discards it, stirring the pulp with one raw, chapped hand.

"It wasn't your fault," he says.

"That's not what you said before," she whispers, and the mold and deckle fall into the vat as she covers her face with her hands.

"I was wrong," he says. "God, I was wrong. I'm so, so

Emily Hess
Elizabethtown, PA

sorry."

She drops her hands from her face and retrieves the mold and deckle from the vat, methodically picking strands of sisal from the frame as she whispers "What if you weren't wrong? What if I, what if there's something wrong with me, or something I did, or—I felt her move, Nathan. She was perfect. What if—what if it happens again and I lose another baby and, Nathan, I can't, I can't." She's shaking, knuckles white against the deckle's damp wood.

He takes the frame from her hands, lays it on the table. He takes her in his arms; she lays her cheek against his chest.

"Nathan?"

"Yes?" he murmurs; she can feel the movement of his lips and his warm breath against her scalp.

She slips out of his embrace and moves to her workbench, takes the mold and deckle, squares the edges. She dips the frame into the sisal pulp, pulling a sheet and examining it. The sheet is uneven, one tangled fiber edge thick and sloped above the other. She turns the frame and kisses the mesh against the surface of the vat so the sheet falls free. She mixes the fibers with her hand, long strands slipping between her fingers. "I, I'm afraid," she says, softly, watching her hands as she pulls another sheet. She couches the sheet onto the felt, pressing a bubble in the paper with her index finger.

He watches as she moves through the process, pulling and couching, charging the vat with more sisal and thickener, making papers until the post is a thick layered sandwich of damp felts and sheets.

"Let me," he says as she strains to lift the heavy pile on its wooden board. He takes the pile from her hands and carries the post to the hydraulic press. He pumps the handle, pressing the pile, and water spills over the edge onto his black leather shoes.

They transfer the sheets to the drying boards, sticking

Emily Hess
Elizabethtown, PA

the paper to the formica laminate and rolling them flat with rubber brayers. The sunlight coming through the window and skylight will dry the sheets, pulling out the water until the sisal's long blonde fibers glimmer with a rosy luster.

"I'm afraid," she says again, running a finger around the squared edges of a sheet, checking its adherence to the board. "I don't want to lose another baby." She takes the stack of empty felts and distributes them over the board, where their damp weight will keep the papers flat as they dry and prevent cockling.

She walks to him, slips her dry, chapped hand into his. Breathing in the scent of his aftershave, the faint aroma of cedar and jojoba and bay, she traces her thumb down his jaw, wiping away the smear of shaving cream. "Nathan, I can't bear to lose another baby. But..." She looks at him, her husband, in his grey suit and his damp shoes, the sun from the skylight gilding his blond hair with the same rosy luster as the drying sisal. "But I can't bear to lose you either," she says.

***

Lyn Lifshin
Vienna, VA

The Heron in Snow

floating above the
water and suddenly
into the blue of snow.
The whiteness stuns,
fresh, without scars
as for that moment
I felt new, myself,
undamaged, new

Sherry B. Hanson
Portland, OR

Cannonade

Deep in the night I am four and my mother
takes me to the window, see the lights
across the bay, hear the cannonading surf

back in bed, back to sleep beside my sister,
magic time, summer at Uncle's house by the sea.

From the first wave that rolled on earth
the grandfathers speak of fish
like forks of lightning at the nets,
sky luminous and soaked in fire,
a billion stars shining brightly
in a child's dreams. They speak also

of fracture. When the plates shift
and bring rising wind and mountainous seas,
sheets of rain drumming the sands,
I find myself knee-deep, foam sucking my ankles.

Let us speak again of my sister as we come on
black ledges and the quicksand of nightmare.

Hunched against the wind, morning brings the worst.

With her space gone dark I must look
on the rain as holy,
lightning flickering the horizon as her elegy.
She loved the cannonade, this perfect altar piece.
It is fitting the sea will seine her ashes forever.

Paul G. Charbonneau
Rockport, ME

Christmas Eve Over Penobscot Bay

Tightly lined together
under the pitched roof of a place
called Children's Chapel,
we watch beyond the bay
a distant flash give us
a green light
to dare follow our hearts

while the vast sea mingles
with a sky barely lit
by December's moon
as it seemingly exhales
a holy breath on us all,
inspiriting us to pursue light
no matter how dim it seems.

And so we sing
to the beat of waves
waking us to hear
the stirrings
of Eternal Being.

P. C. Moorehead
North Lake, WI

Surf-Dashed

I am surf-dashed,
surf-dashed,
pounded
by waves
of sorrow,
of longing.

I want the shore—
that longed for
place of peace.

I want to lie there
in the sand
and be.

***

Headwaters

It rushed at me from the headwaters of my life—
a rapid current, flowing through me, encircling me.

I grabbed for a rock.
There was none.

I lay back and accepted the swirling darkness
as it whirled about, engulfing me, charging me with its pain.

The terrible rush slowed, then distanced.
The calm eddy surrounded me.

Mara Borer
Webster City, IA

Rescued

Airless. The walls of wood and care close in
And wrap themselves around my heart.
The cry that pounds and echoes through my brain
Threatens to burst my smothered soul apart.

I shake within the darkness, shiver close
As blackened fog clouds my eyes and head.
But yet, an ever trustful instinct guides me
Out to the door, to where the sunlight treads.

A wind
Breathes upon my face like a phantom kiss, to blow away my
        tears.
The air cleanses my lungs of the stain of sin
And carries it away into the expanse of sky,
To fade like a butterfly's wing.
The trees murmur the words of angels,
Words that mere humans cannot understand,
But that whisper to a tiny human soul
Like mine.
With each step, I trace
The many paths of the little ant
And wonder if the grasses comfort him
As the trees nourish me.
The sun upon my face
Burns away the festering sores upon my heart
And fills me with the peace of morning rain
And blooming petals
And birdsong.
I stretch my hand, as in thanksgiving, and I know
That I am saved,
And I am whole.

A. McKinne Stires
Westport Island, ME

Shorter Shadows

Hear the soil breath again, its heavy blanket
stripped away by a warming sun.
Beneath a spruce bow, the last snow patch
melts in trickles over leaf dams
into swimming pools for springtails.

Smell the wet, cramped earth promising survival
in the coming year. Crocuses inch out
from under their covers, stretch their emerald arms,
open purple mouths, and yawn with silent,
yellow throats in the sunlight.

Echoing from the marsh, through naked trees,
blackbirds boast and gossip, and straighten
their colored handkerchiefs. Old brown around our house
turns green, as frost gives way to drying.

Winter's hold recedes
with shorter shadows,
shorter woodpiles
and shorter nights.

Rena C. Winters
Las Vegas, NV

Bob Hope—Patriot

It seemed that he had always been there like a part of our family. First it was his radio shows, next his motion pictures and then television where he came into every home in the USA. He was known as America's greatest showman and that's true. However, he could also be called America's greatest patriot because of the millions of lives he touched through his endless USO tours where he entertained, bringing hope, joy and laughter to American combat troops at the front lines and in the hospitals. His devotion to his country and the men and women who served in the armed forces was unlimited.

Bob mastered every comic venue: vaudeville, Broadway, radio, movies and television, and over his career collected hundreds of humanitarian awards. However, his greatest accomplishment was his unfailing response to the USO and providing entertainment for our military forces on all its battlefields and in all its wars for over half a century.

The troops loved him and so did the families of the military men and women back home.

Although a member of the mostly jaded entertainment industry, I would always feel the chills go up and down my spine when I would see Bob and his current troupe at some front line military outpost or hear him sing "Thanks for the Memory." Then, out of the blue, my job put me in contact with Bob and the USO.

In 1980 I was writer and associate producer of the ninety minute special "My Little Corner of the World." This show was designed with a heavy dose of "Americana" that included long segments devoted to the United States Military Academy at West Point. These included the West Point Corps of Cadets in a special dress parade in honor of General William C. Westmoreland who was also interviewed. An outstanding

Rena C. Winters
Las Vegas, NV

performance by the famous West Point Glee Club and a review of the football eras of Glenn Davis, Felix "Doc" Blanchard and Peter Dawkins, all of them Heisman Trophy winners.

Other segments included the advent of jazz and gospel, truly America's gift to the world of music coming up the Mississippi from New Orleans to Chicago then spreading throughout the land.

The smashing climax, that won vast critical acclaim, was shot during a rain storm at historic Valley Forge, the Nation's Shrine, with the historic Medal of Honor Grove serving as the background.

However, something vital was missing. It was Bob Hope and his famous USO military tours. I picked up the phone and called Bob's headquarters in Toluca Lake, California hoping to speak to one of his assistants. The minute I mentioned the USO Bob was on the line asking what he could do for me.

I told him that the show was about America and I didn't want to do the show without spotlighting him and his work with the USO. With his heavy schedule it was impossible for him to join our cast and crew at West Point but he would be happy to package film clips from his visits to troops in Vietnam including a heartwarming Christmas Eve performance with Les Brown and his Orchestra plus the famous stars that went on that trip. As a major plus he would go into the studio and film a special salute to our show and the USO. I held my breath when I asked what his fee would be, then I heard that famous Bob Hope laugh. "Honey we're not going to talk about fees. This for the USO and America."

As promised, the clips and his special salute arrived a few days later. He was celebrating his silver anniversary with the USO. Twenty-five years of performances around the world.

When we edited our show, Bob's clips and USO salute fit perfectly. The American public responded to the program and it was awarded the Freedoms Foundation and American

Rena C. Winters
Las Vegas, NV

Family Heritage Awards.

I returned the film to Bob at his headquarters before the show was released to thank him for his help. He was the same man I had watched since childhood. Warm and funny taking time to thank us for having him when it was really the other way around.

Bob Hope, a man for all seasons left us when he was 100.

I miss him. His talent, his warmth and his eternal giving of himself to the USO and America's military. I don't think there will ever be another like him. Greatest entertainer and a super patriot who proved over and over again how much he loved this wonderful country.

Our country, yours and mine, our little corner of the world.

***

Corinne Davis
Montpelier, VT

Serenity

There is no other place that I would rather be
Than here in this park, just you and me
So intensely quiet that there is no sound
Except for our footsteps on this snow covered ground
The towering trees surround us as if in an embrace
And we welcome the snowflakes as they tickle our face
Walk with me and hold my hand
And be content knowing that you are part of God's plan
Lights shimmering all around for as far as we can see
The moon reflecting itself off
The icy covered branches of the trees
Where else could one possibly want to be
Than in this place of serenity

Joan Peck Arnold
South Berwick, ME

Blood Red Letters

for Tara

The natural order capsizes
and an ever-expanding dark puddle
is pooling under my door
growing and growing
until it has almost reached
my lopsided chair. I howl to
the most distant galaxies
why and wherefore
but get a dearth of answers
just as I knew it would be.
A dead weight has moved in
has laid its tonnage
on my shoulders. Every sinew
within me aches.
Salt has dried on my face
until it has crevassed into furrows.
I can taste the ache, the salt
feel them scar my heart
her name burned there in darker
than blood red letters

Kate Leigh
Portsmouth, NH

Waking Up in a Cozy Tent

Waking up in a cozy tent
Is a dreamlike pleasure, when
The bough of pine drapes
Across the entrance flap,
And all the bugs you see
Through sleepy eyes are
On the outside of the mesh,
You can hear the birds
Ignoring the tent, going
About their habits of
Feeding and eating, the world
You are not ready for,
You just lie still and
Aware, burrowed into
A flannel-lined bag with
Your knees tucked up.

***

Let It Unfold

Hesitant and fearful to fall asleep
As if my dreams can bring me to grief.
Locked in a dark dance of tearful grace,
Worse couplets haunt me during the days.
'Tis fantasy, all this life with its woes,
I'll never encompass that anything goes.
Take it all serious, swallow it whole,
I wake with awareness, let it unfold.

Susann Pelletier
Lewiston, ME

Account

Autumn:
Bounty falls in a single night's wind.
Now, the apples await, glance
Upwards their reds, their greens
From the ground.

I will take account of this beauty left—
Pick the best of the bruised—
Drops.
At dusk, wild turkeys emerge from the shades
        of poplar, ash, grape
Stride in their twilight trance
        up slope to the grove.

Night now,
Daughter, let me tell you the sum of my day:
Gathered a bushel of apples,
Saw thirteen turkeys, then a flock of robins and
Two companion flickers on the bank.
(O how the red blazed on their heads!)
The afternoon was warm, but already birch leaves scatter
On the patio, under my feet...
So many bees were gathering on the mint
(I could not cut it down!)
The blossoms like little spires of mauve,
And the bees buzzing late prayers there,
In this last land of milk and honey

I remembered
How the big maple shed a million leaves
How you and I raked them up into an expansive heap

(continued)

Susann Pelletier
Lewiston, ME

Of yellows and reds
(They are late falling this year.)
How you jumped in; I reclined.
We smelled the woodsmoke from the Alden's,
And the dropped apples close by,
The wool in our sweaters.
I held your damp hand;
Touched your cold cheek, red, to mine.
Do you remember what autumn gave you, gave me?
Do you remember the streaked apples,
O their reds, their greens!

***

Bereft

The widow bends in an April wind,
Picks up the limbs and twigs
The old maple let go last night.
Above her, the tree boasts again,
Thousands of leaf buds, reddening,
Even from branches she'd imagined dead.

The sky this morning offers her its blue
But she will not look up,
Only down, to hard shades of brown,
To branches that fell,
And startled in the dark,
As did her tears in their three seasons
Apart.

Back stooped, she'll work until the work
Is done.
And when she tires, she will not lean
On the tree's trunk.

Karen E. Wagner
Ashland, MA

Pulling Lobster Traps

Rocking in the rough
waters off Cape Neddick
hauling in lobster traps,
catch mostly undersized,
gulls screeching overhead,
makes me think of when
lobsters crawled ashore
in the pilgrim settlements,
became fodder for the pigs
no trap necessary,
so plentiful the harvest.
Not fit for human
consumption, the
ugly crustaceans
ranked
suitable for scavengers
with other ocean trash,
the pigs grew fat,
off today's delicacies.
Leaves me wondering
how long before barnacles
are valued as an
epicurean delight?

John T. Hagan
Springboro, OH

A Highland Halloween

Finishing my most recent short story one late Halloween afternoon on my Highland County horse farm, I saddled my spirited but gentle mare, Sally, fully expecting a languorous ride into the twilight. Sally, a striking fifteen-hand sorrel, is one of three Quarter Horse mares on the farm, two of which belong to me, and the third I board for a neighboring high school student for whom I occasionally serve as a writing tutor.

Neither Sally nor my other mare, Sadie, had been ridden in over a week, and the aromatic and unseasonably warm autumn air beckoned us to the riding trail. Once brushed, saddled, and bridled, Sally allowed me the barest time to find both stirrups before she pranced from the barn, through the barnyard, and down the hill next to the paddock toward the creek. I gave Sally her head, and she cantered along the trail between the front bean field on the left and the wooded creek line on the right. The October colors were in grand profusion, and the wind jitterbugged through the trees, making the leaves a kaleidoscope of sundry designs and dazzling hues. I had been so busy with my fiction writing and barn renovations throughout the fall that I had not appreciated the magnificent foliage now gracing the rolling topography of the land. Astride a thousand pounds of horseflesh, however, I found my senses awakening to the tactile stimuli beneath and around me. Rather than take the loop to the left and head in a general direction back toward the barnyard, I extended the ride significantly by taking a more circuitous route across the wondering spring-fed stream.

Crossing the sandy creek bed, Sally lunged up the craggy bank and into the fallow field above, and then we headed toward the remnants of the old "house in the holler" that once served as temporary living quarters for itinerant field

John T. Hagan
Springboro, OH

workers when the farm was vastly larger than its current ninety acres and sustained all manner of grains and live-stock.

"C'mon, Sally, let's circle the old house on the buggy lane."

The buggy lane was actually a nineteenth-century county road used by family doctors, traveling salesmen, and casual visitors to reach remote farmhouses and residents, but it had long ago been integrated into the present farmstead. We loped across the former tobacco field and entered the buggy lane that was now just a tractor run taking us up the steep hill and opening into a five-acre hay field that provided a panoramic and vibrant view of the farm.

"I wish we could freeze this vision and moment, Sally girl! Take a mental picture with me before we head back to the barn."

Sally nickered in what seemed to be an affirmation of her mutual appreciation of the scene before we descended the hill on our roundabout return trip. We picked up the pace a bit because I hoped to avoid total darkness during the some-what perilous rutting season, and we were soon heading up the quarter-mile gravel lane toward the house and barn. Before ending this serene and almost surreal horseback ride, I decided to pull Sally off the lane and direct her along a branch of the bridle trail that wound through a dense wood-lot, which simply begged to be traveled, notwithstanding the imminent darkness. What may have unconsciously prompt-ed my deviation was the faint but now growing aroma of burning leaves and logs. As we started up the hill, Sally shied twice before I began to hear what she had obviously detected. At her first reluctance, I had thought she smelled or heard the presence of deer, which would invariably cause her anxiety, but I soon began to hear the faintest sounds of human voices somewhere beyond our vision among the trees. Rounding a bend in the woods, I could see in the dusk a group of four figures seated on logs and stumps in a rough

John T. Hagan
Springboro, OH

circle around a campfire, and the sight augured for me a gathering of goblins on this Halloween night.

"Easy, Sally girl, easy," I half-whispered to my equine pal, trying more to assure myself than my mount.

I approached the figures apprehensively and halted Sally about twenty feet from their seated location. As the dancing flames erratically illuminated these figures, I beheld four of the most curiously attired men I had ever seen. Not one deigned to acknowledge me; so casting caution aside, I stepped down from Sally and walked toward them in a most deferential manner, though I was vexed by the gall of these intrusive masqueraders.

"Good evening, gentlemen. Might I inquire as to what you're doing in these woods and why you're keeping a campfire at this time on my property?"

They continued to murmur among themselves, ignoring me as if I were no more than a hoot owl on a sycamore branch down in the marshes.

"Excuse me, gentlemen. I don't mean to appear inhospitable, but I'd like to know what you're doing here on Halloween night in my woods. If you need assistance, I'll gladly help, but as the proprietor of this farm I believe I'm owed an explanation of your intentions."

After a disconcerting delay, a gangling, sunken-faced, and long-nosed fellow rose from his stump-seat and addressed me rather disdainfully. He was about 6'3" but seemed to weigh no more than 170 pounds. He was attired in a white shirt and neckerchief, black waistcoat and jacket, black pants and colonial boots, and a velvet three-cocked hat.

"My good man, you are in the company of four renowned travelers whose stories are the stuff of legend. We are en route to Oxford, Mississippi, where we intend to enroll at Ole Miss University under the provisions there for designated citizens, and we'll then collaborate on the great American novel. We sojourn in this sylvan setting tonight to plan the balance

John T. Hagan
Springboro, OH

of our itinerary and to begin preliminary discussions of what will be our timeless tome.”

“Tell ’im, Ichabod,” said a raspy voice behind the billowing pipe smoke below the standing figure.

To say the temerity and attire of this indignant fellow took me aback fails to render my amazement. Said I, while gathering my composure, “You’re not Ichabod Crane of Sleepy Hollow fame are you?”

“He is, young fellow, and it might behoove you to hear our stories and learn the reason for our journey together,” interjected the white-bearded kibitzer who then resumed puffing on his Little Ladle tavern pipe.

This odd-looking smoker wore a black Puritan hat, a bright blue coat with cuffed sleeves, yellow knickers, white knee-length stockings, and brown high-topped shoes with buckles.

The imperious splinter of a man resumed, seemingly annoyed by his companion’s interruption.

“You’ve apparently heard of me, Mister...”

“Shannon, Mike Shannon,” I said quickly. “I...I own this place.”

“Yes...yes, you told us that. Since you know something of me, Mr. Shannon, I hasten to tell you that theories of my demise at the hands of the headless Hessian are very much in error. True, that Philistine Abraham “Brom Bones” Van Brunt did pursue me as I made my way from the Van Tassel farm on the rambunctious Gunpowder that storied night, but the pumpkin he hurled from his steed sailed over my head and struck a nearby tree. Having lost out to “Bones” in my pursuit of the hand and wealth of the beautiful Katrina Van Tassel, I quit Sleepy Hollow as a schoolmaster immediately and returned covertly in the night to my roots on the Hudson Eastern Shore. Since then I have earned my bread as an itinerant teacher, and taking my philosophy of ‘Spare the rod and spoil the child’ with me, I have often applied the ferule I now hold to the backsides of reluctant scholars. I have lived

John T. Hagan
Springboro, OH

off the largesse of small country villages until the residents figured out...er, decided that my pedagogy was not the equal of my sustenance. I have, however, made the close acquaintance of many a comely maiden during my travels."

"So, you really are Ichabod Crane!"

"That's right Mr. Shannon, and perhaps you've heard of me," said the puffer.

"Everyone's heard a you Rip," said a third figure seated on a log with his left leg extended to the right of the smoker. He was a youthful specimen in a dark-blue, single-breasted frock coat that bore several brass buttons down its front and was girded by a wide leather belt clasped by an equally wide brass buckle with a *bas-relief* U.S. on it. His sky-blue trousers were tucked into mid-calf, black infantry boots; and his long, flaxen hair was swept back under a rumpled, navy-blue kepi cap with the insignia of two crossed rifles on the front and top.

"I daresay that you know a bit of my story as well," continued the resolute old gent, as he tapped the embers from the clay pipe on his knee and then loaded two more logs on to the flickering fire. He stood for the first time and stepped closer to the blaze, rubbing his hands in a warming action.

"I'm a British-American villager of Dutch descent and a rather skilled raconteur, if I do say so myself. Quite likely, you've heard that Rip Van Winkle was a man who loathed profitable labor, but I submit to you that the pensive, indolent man who'll take a drop now and then is much more of a social asset than the man who's in perpetual pursuit of filthy lucre."

"Well," I started to say, "I have read that..."

"Please don't interrupt my apologia, young man. Where are your manners?"

"Uh...sorry!"

At this point, he withdrew from his inner coat pocket a pewter flask and quaffed a healthy slug of its contents. Wiping his lips on his sleeve, he continued.

John T. Hagan
Springboro, OH

"You probably heard that while fleeing a termagant wife one fall Saturday afternoon, I and my faithful coon dog, Wolf, hiked into the Catskills, seeking relief from her relentless carping. Happening upon some diminutive fellows who were playing at ninepins, I joined them for some comradeship and grog. I believe they may have been some of Henry Hudson's crew, but that's another story. Of course, I'm sure you know that I fell asleep from the effects of their brew and slept for twenty years. And it was a peaceful slumber at that. Now, I want you to know that because a man eschews the back-breaking labor of the noble husbandman and prefers the company of his doting hound to his pitiless spouse does not mean he is remiss as a citizen. I often regaled the youngsters of the village with my fanciful tales, and I was always at the ready to help any neighbor with his farm work, especially if he happened to keep a flagon of rum on the premises. Those of my predispositions are the dessert of society not its castor oil."

He sat back down and took another pull on his flask before scooping some tobacco from his pocket and into the bowl of his pipe. With his rekindled pleasure in hand, he winked at Ichabod, who nodded in obvious approval of his companion's account.

"Well," I said, "you have both removed any misunderstandings regarding your lives and experiences, but..."

"Ya ain't hered all our steries yet, mister!" interjected the figure seated to the right of the young man in blue. He was most unkempt, and he reeked of stale whiskey even in the fragrant woods. He wore a filthy slouch hat over long, twisted black hair, and his buttonless coat hung open, revealing a pair of ragged overalls and a grimy shirt that looked on-loan from Ezekiel, son of Buzi. His long, salt-and-pepper beard provided all the creature comforts sought by judicious cooties.

"Now hold on, Pap," said blue boy. "You'll get your turn, but I'd like to know if this gentleman has heard of me."

John T. Hagan
Springboro, OH

"And you are..."

"Henry. Henry Fleming," said the earnest young man as he stood and placed a bandanna on the stump-seat behind him.

"Fleming...Henry Fleming. Let me think," I said.

"Does the Civil War help you any?"

"Are you..."

"Yes, I am. And no doubt you probably hold me in very low regard. As a callow eighteen-year-old, I volunteered for the 304th New York during the Civil War. I was filled with a sense of patriotism and glory, and I, of course, couldn't wait to see some of that celebrated action. Naturally, prior to the first engagement, I began to see the very real and imminent danger of battle. As you probably know, I ran from the fight in my craven fear and met retreating and advancing columns as I did. Having engaged a fellow Union soldier aggressively, he struck me with the barrel of his rifle, leaving a bloody gash on the side of my head. As you also probably know, I returned to my battalion, and when my head injury was mistaken for a battle wound, I acquitted myself well from that time on."

"Yes, Henry, we discussed your case each year in my American literature classes when I was teaching high school English. *The Red Badge of Courage* was part of the juniors' required reading."

"Well, quite likely, I was often found derelict in my behavior by your students for running from my first battle, but those young people should know that when the fanfare and falderal that sends us off to war is behind us, we front-line fodder are left with the realization that what lies before us is a bit more meaningful than the 'mom-and-apple-pie' reasons for the grisly slaughter. When boys and men lie on blood-soaked fields watching entrails spill from their bellies, they're no longer fighting for the honor of their mothers, they're bawling for the comfort of their mothers."

A hush fell over the encampment, and no one seemed to

John T. Hagan
Springboro, OH

know when or how to commence conversation. I broke the silence with an affirmation of Henry's insights.

"Actually Henry, our discussions of your reaction were often lively but equally divided. Naturally, the more macho and naïve students were critical of your initial behavior, but even they decided that you redeemed yourself at length for the most part. Others felt like you did what came naturally to an inexperienced youth facing the realities of war. They often said..."

"Lissen 'ere," said a voice from under a dirty slouch hat. "Ya wanna hear suthin' wirth talkin' 'bout, lissen a my stery."

The man in the filthy hat with a lid that flopped open bent down between his knees and brought up a half-gallon, stoneware whiskey jug and took a long pull on its contents. As he bent down again to replace the jug, the lid of his hat flopped open again. He then rose to a precarious semi-upright position to hold court.

"Lotsa folks think I'm sumkinda snake inna grass cuz ol' man Twain made me a shamelis thief, a chile abuser, a drunkin' sot, 'n a hateful bigot. Well, mebbe I am, but all I'z iver wanted wuz ta git my rights. Folks git down on me cuz I uze that N-word now 'n then 'n cuss better'n ol' Sowberry Hagan. Well, I ain't Pap Finn hisself if I don't pervide a pow-erful suhvice ta th' govment."

"Actually, Mr. Finn," I said to this offensive lout, "you made every attempt to steal young Huck's reward money, and your ill-treatment of him is well-documented. Your atti-tude toward the black professor was the essence of racial prejudice."

"Now, ya looky 'ere. That p'fessor thought I wuz jist white trash 'n..."

"That's your opinion, but..."

"Now, hol' on a minute and don't innerrupt. My pint is that Twain feller used me as a lowdown shiflis skunk ta show 'is readers th' ugliness of th' prejudice tha' galls you so. He made me an example awat not ta be. That sneaky scundrl

John T. Hagan
Springboro, OH

had all th' ugliness of bigotry comin' outta my pie hole. So, I'm jinin' these fellers ta make my case 'n hep 'em set record straight in th' book we're writin'."

About that time, Pap started listing to the right, so Henry Fleming guided the eloquent self-defender to his seat where he resumed a mouth-to-mouth love affair with his jug.

"It seems, gentlemen," I began, "that I have fallen upon a troupe of transients who have captured my fancy. You see, I'm a bit of a journeyman writer myself, and a retired teacher, Mr. Crane. With your permission, I'd be delighted, honored in fact, to accompany all of you to Mississippi and hear more of your stories along the way. I couldn't tarry long in Oxford, of course, but I would certainly take two or three weeks away from the farm to enrich my literary insights and gain immeasurable grist for my own stories."

They said nothing at first, but then they all leaned in toward the fire and began a muffled confab. In the meantime, Sally, whom I had nearly forgotten, was waiting in abeyance. She actually began nudging me with her nose in a not-so-subtle reminder that she wanted to return to the barn and be divest of the saddle. At length, however, Ichabod turned toward me and seemed to speak for the group.

"Mr. Shannon, if we were to take you with us, you'd need to understand that we'll be traveling clandestinely and often under cover of darkness."

"Oh yes. I certainly understand your need to remain under the radar."

"Under the...radar?"

"Under cover; that is, unseen or undetected."

"Yes, yes. But how would you manage your affairs, your farm while you were away?"

"I tutor a neighbor boy and board his horse, and he'd be delighted to earn some spending money and keep his horse here cost-free for the month of November by looking after the horses and tending to the house and barn."

John T. Hagan
Springboro, OH

Ichabod leaned in to the huddle again and whispered some comments. At length, he stood once more and said, "Mr. Shannon, we have decided to take you along. Since you have an affinity for writing, we would ask that you chronicle our trip and note the desirable or beneficial traits in us that may not have emerged in our oft-studied stories."

"I'll be ready in the morning. Will you be staying here in the woods tonight?"

"Indeed, we will, but mind you, we'll be leaving before dawn. You'll need to join us no later than 5:00 a.m. You'll also need a knapsack with your provisions for the journey."

"No problem. I have everything I need for backpacking."

"Backpacking?"

"Traveling by foot."

"We shall expect you before daybreak, Mr. Shannon. Be sure to bring pencil and tablet."

"I will, and good-night!"

"Good-night, Mr. Shannon!" the group said in chorus.

I swung a leg over Sally, and we picked our way back to the barn. I turned her out quickly and hurried to the house, where I called Cameron and told him what I needed over the next three weeks or so. Then I packed clothes, provisions, and materials into my backpack and began planning the fascinating travel journal I would compile with these escapees from the pages of classics. By the time I crawled into bed, I heard one o'clock strike on the grandfather clock down in the foyer. I probably did not fall asleep until after two.

When I opened my eyes again, the sunlight was streaming through my bedroom window. My alarm clock, set for 4:30 had not gone off. It was now 5:55. In my excitement, I had not pulled the pin to activate the alarm mode before I had fallen asleep. I threw on my clothes and grabbed my backpack and a Gatorade. I raced back to the woods, frantic that I had held up the group. When I reached the familiar spot where they had camped the night before, they were not only gone, but not one sign of a campfire could I find.

John T. Hagan
Springboro, OH

"That's weird," I said aloud. "I can understand that they left without me, but how did they dispose of all remnants of the fire?"

As I began a closer inspection, I discovered that also missing were the stumps and logs that my mysterious friends had sat upon, and there were no footprints or any signs of a recent gathering. Suddenly, the cold realization befell me that I had either been hallucinating or dreaming.

"You fool," I said to myself, "what would make you think you were actually going to take a walking trip to Mississippi with four fictional characters?"

I sat down on a large rock and began to laugh at my own foolishness. After much reflection and rationalization, I concluded that the apple cider I had been drinking to slake a thirst during my previous day's writing session must have been laced with brandy or rum.

"Yes, that was it. Old man Jessup must have slammed some hooch into that batch, and I was three-sheets-to-the-wind without knowing it."

I rose to pick up my backpack and return to the farmhouse. Taking a final look about me, I noticed something peculiar at the base of a large, nearby poplar tree. There, lying together, I found a Little Ladle pipe, a ferule, a half-gallon stoneware jug, and a bloodied bandanna. I froze.

Elmae Passineau
Weston, WI

Fair Trade

The cucumbers were big
   the bucket was small
   just three fit into that pail
   heavy enough for a toddler...
   and Grandpa paid a nickel

The shiny silver coin was pretty
   but its true value was in the penny candy
   at Omernik's Grocery Store

Lemon drops, root beer barrels,
licorice twists, Mary Janes,
Bit O' Honeys, peppermint sticks,
marshmallow cones, Turkish taffy,
Tootsie Rolls, butterscotch buttons...

Mr. Omernik delicately dropped
   my five carefully selected sweets
   into a small brown paper bag,
   leaned forward,
   and solemnly handed it to me
I placed my nickel on his palm,
   our eyes locked,
   a satisfactory transaction, all around

Sylvia Little-Sweat
Wingate, NC

Birth

For months you lay
beneath my heart
which pulsed near yours
in the dark.

My flesh, my bones
were yours to own.

On quiet nights as you
curled within asleep
I thought I sensed infinity.

But soon you caught
life's breath
to live apart from me.

To hold you in my arms
was ultimately to see
life's great improbability—

for neither could I let you go
nor would you let me stay.

Because you have taken
life from me
I now understand
mortality.

Stephen Goldfinger
West Newton, MA

Precepting

Before bringing me to meet her
He abbreviates the reason she's here.
An 80 year old lady, my trainee begins,
Pleasant, fairly intact, brought in by her daughter.
Her problem is constipation
And she's starting to get forgetful.
Hardly a new scenario for either of us.

In the few seconds it takes to reach the examining room
I tailor my persona to fit what I know about her.
Show interest, be lively, smile, listen.
Get her to talk about the highlights of her life
Above all, humor her, poor thing.
How many more years can she have?
And visits to doctors are big things
At a certain age.

She is small, slumped in her seat
White hair well-combed, skin wrinkled,
Winning smile, proud of her new teeth that fit so well.
I like this grandma (possibly great grandma)
Flatter her, make her feel important, joke a bit about her
          infirmities.
Make a few suggestions along the way.
Really want her to feel good.
Some would call it condescending.
I call it good care.
People her age need that extra show of interest.
They deserve it.

Stephen Goldfinger
West Newton, MA

I leave the room knowing things went well.
That's the way I want to be treated some day when I reach
her age.
And only then does it dawn on me.
In forty-six days my family will gather
To celebrate my eightieth birthday.

***

Sylvia Little-Sweat
Wingate, NC

Sea Change

At the salt marsh rim
an egret stands and scans
the shallow brine
as the iridescent tide laps
and sucks the grassy reeds.
Its beak condenses sunlight
shimmery as the sea.

To eat an oyster from its shell
or see a turtle dig the sand
to lay her eggs then lumber
back to sea is to swim again
in tidal salt, borne by primal
need to be cast ashore to nest
like a turtle or to stand
in fecund mud like an egret
waiting
waiting
to taste
the teeming sea.

Jean Biegun
Manitowoc, WI

Stations of Lent

I've been thinking about sin lately,
the push of black and white hats in the world.
Here at Supercuts waiting for a trim,

I watch new piles of clippings
get swept up by Kori, my confessor this month.
She murmurs soft sympathy while intuiting

my crimes: *No, the kids won't be home*
for Easter, too busy, no time to call even
...you know how it is these days.

My gray hairs fall on the cape around my neck,
DNA strands spiraled tightly in each snip,
the sins of the fathers and mothers,

generations that still keep growing from my head.
Kori has blessed me with a clean look this time.
I pull my knit cap down to keep warm

and hurry to the Full Canteen next door
for coffee and another try for forgiveness
of flashbacks in black and white hats.

Trudy Wells-Meyer
Scottsdale, AZ

NORMAL...the Meaning of One Simple Word

To live with fear for days is what makes elation seem a brand new feeling....

The morning I walked into that place that hurts women for a living, for a mammogram I didn't believe in getting, my thoughts were carefree, my face smiling. My over confident mind planned to get-it-over-with fast, hoping it would not take up too much of my organized day ahead. It was Monday, my day off. My instincts had taken over and I no longer ignored my doctor's orders; it had been many years. I had actually called and made an appointment. I disregarded my health-nut beliefs, for years, knowing health is a choice, a story for another time.

No man will ever know what a woman goes through on the way to that controversial mammogram appointment. What a woman's mind does to her brain, wondering about all the possibilities that can happen to one of the most womanly body parts—her breasts. To face possibly missing a most visual part of her body; can anyone truly relate to that? The pain of a mammogram, the squeezing hard and flattening of a breast, a machine that does not seem to know when to stop. It's like being attacked by a robot. What about having to grab your breast and lay it on a shelf designed to accommodate your height, your size, all the while you listen to a nurse in charge, "Higher, more to the left." Over where? Anxious moments lasting too long, simply is no fun.

I undressed to the waist, put on a flowered blue gown and pulled it tight, trying to ignore my dislike for blue. An extremely friendly young girl with smiling eyes showed me to the exam-room, a tiny dark room. The dreaded picture-tak-

Trudy Wells-Meyer
Scottsdale, AZ

ing machine looked huge. Nurse Wretched was waiting. A middle-aged, unsmiling, overweight woman with hair that matched her mood, an early Monday-morning-sour-behavior like as a weekend gone badly. In her irritated voice she informed me to put my breast, where, on what? You sure, up there? She had forgotten to lower that famous mammogram shelf where countless breasts have gone before me.

"How long has your nipple been inverted?"

"My what?" I mumbled.

She repeated the question in a voice that seemed to have awakened.

 "Sorry," I answered. "I don't make a habit of looking at my nipple. I am now to look at my nipples? What happened to check for a lump?" I know I sounded flustered, because I was.

I could feel the smile on my face fade when I heard her say, "An inverted nipple is not a good sign."

An eerie silence filled the room as she continued the exam. Fearful speculations started to rise. They were abruptly interrupted after Wretched checked with a frown and looked at the pictures closely. It was my right breast. Finally, with a quiver in my voice I dared to ask,

"What does an inverted nipple mean?"

I heard her say in a harsh business-like voice, "There usually is something going on in there...." Her facial expression said **Cancer**, as did my racing thoughts.

To cover an unfamiliar nervousness and near trembling, I put my hand on my heart. I took a deep breath. I told myself to breathe because this was one of those moments where you could easily stop. I tried to act nonchalant.

On the way out Nurse Wretched said in her stern voice that seemed like shouting, "Your doctor will have the result today. She will read it tomorrow and let you know."

Why the urgency? I was too dazed to ask that follow-up question.

With sinking feelings I walked to my car. I raised my eyes

Trudy Wells-Meyer
Scottsdale, AZ

to heaven in a classic expression of disbelief. I raced home. I couldn't wait to call my gynecologist's office, my doctor, (a woman), to ask a question I never thought about or heard of, "What does an inverted nipple mean?" I dialed the number with such haste I missed a number. I redialed, only to get a recording: Their vacation had started, today, for ten days. I must have looked downright ill. Now what? Scrambled thoughts flew around in my brain. *Who will read my test? And clearly, when?*

Life seemed to slow to a crawl as the minutes filled with worries. The texture of reality underwent a dramatic change. A fear known to all women enveloped me. It seemed to be my turn. I called the emergency number that was given on their vacation-message, only to talk to another answering machine. I explained my problem with a voice that didn't seem my own, listened to by whom? No call back!

The cold hard side of life was testing my daily smile. A huge cloud had formed. Lost in my thoughts I listened to the sounds of silence, wondering will my life ever be the same again. Cursing silently my gut feeling that drove me to make an appointment for a mammogram; no longer ignoring my doctor's order seemed to be totally the wrong time. In a few days we were leaving for a most anticipated trip to Europe for three weeks.

Spring in Paris, the city of lights; it was May in Arizona.

Our amazing trip included visiting my family in Switzerland, and a class reunion in my tiny home town where I grew up. A trip with countless, prearranged dates and times to see friends and family in various cities; even traveling to the Italian Alps, a long overdue invitation to visit my favorite and only uncle in his high-up-in-the-mountain summer home.

Our return to Paris, traveling on the TGV, a high-speed train from Switzerland was first on our list, Paris, our honeymoon destination thirty six years ago.

Trudy Wells-Meyer
Scottsdale, AZ

Cloud nine in a ditch...for now.

I called the office again, leaving the news of my seemingly huge problem on the emergency number answering machine. Again, nobody called me back. Was my problem not severe enough for the courtesy of a call-back for me to ask someone who knew something? Mentally exhausted I left one last message on that detested recording. I yelled I would call from Paris as soon as they were back in the office. It appeared the only thing I could do. I hung up with a huge sigh, seeking warmth from a chill only I could feel. The sense of powerlessness made me feel faint.

In the days that followed that fateful morning of dreadful news, in my mind I tried to instant-replay every word the nurse had said, hoping I would find something, anything I may have missed to make it all less serious. I searched intently for some news about an inverted nipple (internet) fearful of what I might find. I talked to people, anybody.

The one I wished I hadn't confided in was my neighbor. She blurted out in words too loud, "Oh yes, my mother-in-law had an inverted nipple. She wouldn't go to the doctor for months. She died because of a tumor in her breast."

Did I stumble on the truth, only to wish I hadn't?

While I was packing and for days to come I lived in the prison of my nights and days. On the flight to Zürich Switzerland, changing planes in Atlanta, nine long hours on a plane across the Atlantic, to worry about breast cancer, a restless night no doubt. Sleep did not come; yet, high up in the air I felt close to God. The quiet in my heart was immeasurable. In the early morning I looked out at the majestic sunrise over the Swiss Alps and stared at the momentary brilliance up in the sky emerging through the clouds. I closed my eyes with a sob, blinking, not to miss this entire splendor in the sky. I will not forget the cold echoing calm like the icy

Trudy Wells-Meyer
Scottsdale, AZ

silence of the high Alps that surrounded me. Several times I found myself looking up to heaven with hope that was more than a wish—it was a silent prayer.

The most unexpected moments in life make one appreciate anything—anything at all. Feeling down and close to despair, an amazing calmness happened, almost like a surrender-close-to-God-feeling, knowing the future is in His hands. Always!

What will be will be....

"Yesterday is history...tomorrow is a mystery...today is a gift."

The word *normal*, through a phone line from Arizona to Paris, it was dinner-time in France, a most clear sound like an echo indelibly imprinted in my mind.

I shouted back, "***NORMAL***?"

The cheerful voice on the other side of the ocean repeated that magnificent word. News of such heart-stopping importance for an instant I could scarcely believe my ears. My jumping off the bed caused my husband Luke to worry; yet, hope in his eyes I heard what I wanted to hear. A piercing sensation I was not prepared for caused my heart to leap and simply filled me with pleasure. I looked at Luke with a silent *wow* on my lips. Left speechless, I realized I was surrounded by feelings I will remember for the rest of my life.

Thank you, God....Are there other words for gratitude? A goose-bump moment! How the power of one word can pave the way to extreme jubilation. Such ecstasy can hardly be put into words. A feeling like music, as I danced around our fancy hotel room, arms stretched up towards heaven; it had taken mere seconds to feel free again. The Eifel Tower in the distance never looked better. The word happy was simply too weak.

Luke's priceless grin got huge. He leaped off his chair and ran towards me with outstretched arms, holding me tight. I listened to the strong beating of his heart...closeness beyond.

Trudy Wells-Meyer
Scottsdale, AZ

It was madly romantic. Happiness shared is truly real.

The clouds in Paris for days had turned to sunshine, literally.

The power of one simple word—***normal***—to hear that glorious word is an elevated moment I am still dizzy from.

A word only, that translated into *the scare is over*...was it?

Five months later I had another test (mammogram) on the breast that worried me sick, and an examination by my doctor. The mystery of my inverted nipple still not truly clear to me; however, I now do look at my nipples on a regular daily basis. When it's *out* I feel ecstatic, when it's *in* the wondering continues. My doctor and various well-informed people have told me for the nipple not to stay in constantly is a real good sign. Only time will tell.

Call for a mammogram!

"Mistakes of the past become the wisdom of the future...."

***

Patrick T. Randolph
Lincoln, NE

Friday Night—1952

A teardrop forming,
Resting in her eye's wet womb;
Birth of a teardrop,

Crawling down her evening face—
Sound of his car—gone again.

the late Anne W. Hammond
Woolwich, ME

Aftermath

The wind is a loud, continuous roar
Tide races water and boats out to sea
The hurricane drops birds who dare to soar.

The storm blasts the bay shore
No place to pause unless the paddler can flea.
The wind is a loud, continuous roar.

A kayak on the bay is no longer laughter galore:
The paddler is scared by limits she cannot see.
The hurricane drops birds who dare to soar.

A black cloud from the west, what will it gore?
Lightening kills on land and windswept sea.
The wind is a loud, continuous roar.

I'm in the kayak. I am the kayak, and more
To fly with the wind, pass the harbor lee.
The hurricane drops birds who dare to soar.

What can the storm bring to personal lore?
A deluded paddler who survives to see reality.
The wind is a loud, continuous roar.
The hurricane drops birds who dare to soar.

Bill Eberle
Thomaston, ME

Haiku for Willow

a beautiful pair
you and my wonderful wife
sleeping together

now when she's away
I bump around by myself:
no cat to talk to

a space filled with you
silently not being there
my heart hears and sees

window is sleeping
sun sparkling on fur no more
table corner mourns

the house is empty
I used to feel our small cat
everywhere at once

house feels less human
our cat is buried outside
inside less of us

forever ever
from eternity to now
paw pads in my mind

Tom Adamson
Fremont, NE

Not Far to Fall

I'm one month short of tomorrow
And yesterday's riding me hard.
I could tell myself the truth
But I'm not ready to play that card.
And then I recall the words
The wise man wrote on my wall,
"You'll survive and you'll arise—

     Because it's not far to fall."

I keep hoping that I'm dreaming,
And I'll wake up, clean and free.
But a highway's out there waiting
And it won't leave without me.
I still hear the gypsy whispering
From behind her twilight shawl,
"From here to the dust, my friend,
     It's just not far to fall."

It was long ago in my early light,
In a place far, far within.
I took the gifts God gave me
And foolishly gave them a spin.
But now I know what I am
In the grand scheme of it all.
I stand smaller than my shadow,
     So it's not far to fall.

Robert B. Moreland
Pleasant Prairie, WI

Late-Night Meditation, Lincoln Memorial

Basked in brilliant neon suns, marble gleams,
calm confidence, "wisdom for the ages" . . .
Seek now, as it comes apart at the seams,
see children die, war on terror rages.

War came in April 1861;
lost half the country in less than six weeks.
Spent four years and countless lives gone, undone
healed endless rifts, renewed hope, justice speaks.

Gettysburg, drafted for minor role there
yet your words fire my heart, stir deep in my soul.
"That these dead shall not have died in vain," dared
"This nation under God," losing control.

"Malice toward none, charity for all,"
God, how we seek "a just and lasting peace"!
Lightening eastern skies, gone now night's pall,
walk to Reflecting Pool, seeking release.

Dew damp grey Wall glistens, pink light of dawn,
fifty flags mirrored in water beyond . . .
Washington Monument upon the lawn,
sweet silence fades as day's bustle responds.

Original citation: Moreland, R.B. "Late Night Meditation, Lincoln Memorial" in Moreland, R.B. and Miner, K.M. *Postcards from Baghdad: Honoring America's Heroes.* Xlibris (Philadelphia, PA, 2008) p100.

Kim Millick
Falmouth, ME

Lying in Wait

I'm now in place. Breathe. Get your heart rate down. Exhale...as slow as possible. Inhale...again. My body is responding, feeling the adrenaline seeping away. Where does adrenaline go when you want to calm yourself, anyway?

I'm perched on a ledge, hiding, with a brook bubbling below my feet. Its flow takes the melting snow downstream, washing the stones bare, too cold for moss to grow. The banks of the stream around me have islands of ice, not yet melted. Relative warmth unlocks the winter's prison sending snowmelt into the brook.

The rocky clay banks of my perch are cold and wet. They smell of frost and mud and mold. *Breathe in. Exhale.* The fresh water has an acidic smell, but clear and cleansing. The deeper waters are cobalt and glacial blue but shallows are transparent to ochre tones. Ripples highlight in hues of creamy whites.

My target is within view. It needs my attention. Through the early morning fog, it lies in wait. Its fur is light as air and teases the fog's misty droplets. They collect on its umber coat lying still like a blanket trying to keep the owner warm and dry. Small and vulnerable, once active and whimsical, it lies still. The envy of thousands, its coat is thick and warm and beautiful. The fur is soft and downy light to the touch just like its ancestors.

The object of my thoughts doesn't need my pity. It's too late. It lies there while I watch and wait. The cold dampness is creeping through the back of my woolen clothes. The air is raw and gnaws at my fingertips. I think forward to when my wait will end. What will I say? What will I do? I don't know who will interrupt my solitude. My disgust for this sport will be evident, no doubt. But who am I more enraged at? The trappers who work hard to tend their traps every day

Kim Millick
Falmouth, ME

and prepare the beautiful pelts? Or those who purchase and adorn themselves in God's creatures? What drives a person to slog their way through the deep snows, take a life in a brutal manner and prepare it for sale? As a warden, I ensure compliance. But my gut objects to this form of taking.

The noise of a snowmobile rudely interrupts the brook's trickling song. It stops within 100 feet of the mink. A man is dressed in brown bulky overalls and large insulated boots looking disproportionately large to his small frame. He is intent on his mission, expertly puts snowshoes on and makes his way to the trap. He has no clue that I am close or watching.

Smiling at his success, he bends over to disengage the harsh metal clamp from its prey. He looks briefly at the creature before placing it in a pouch he's carrying. With no ceremony, he pulls a baggie out with bait to reset the trap for another victim.

"Stop there, sir. Warden!" I bellow. Startled, he raises up to see me but stays silent. "Step away from the trap, sir." I jump across the brook and make my way toward him. He is still and standing now. "You got a weapon on you?"

"No, ma'am, just a club for the critters." The voice of this young man is respectful and slightly shaking. He tries to get a better view of me as I come closer. "Ma'am, you scared the crap out of me. I didn't expect anyone out here."

"I need to see your trapping license and why don't you tell me your name and where you live?" I say as I watch him. He's young, late teens maybe, gangly but spry. He's watching me with quick eyes and concern on his face.

"Wayne. Wayne Toole. I'm a wildlife student at the college; live on campus there....Here's my license."

"You're a wildlife student and a trapper. Have you read the trapping laws, Wayne?"

"Yes, ma'am. I trap to pay for my schoolin'. It takes a lot of pelts to pay for college."

"Regulations say: You ask for permission before you

Kim Millick
Falmouth, ME

cross private property and you put your name and address on your traps. Where's your name on the trap, Wayne? I don't see it, do you?"

Wayne bends over his trap and pushes the snow away from it. "No ma'am. Boy this isn't good. I'm pretty careful about following the law, Warden. I don't want a violation to get in the way of landin' a job at graduation."

"Mark your traps, Wayne, and get permission from the landowners," I say as I begin to write the citation. "So...how's the trapping been this winter?"

"Good. I've done well, which means the population is in good shape."

"I gotta tell you, Wayne, I hate trapping. Seems like a cruel way of taking an animal."

"Yes ma'am, but the population has to have some control or it affects the fish population, farmer's chickens, eggs and the like. I do think it's a sport like hunting. It's man against nature and certainly a part of this country's history. 'Sides, there's a big demand out there. If people were against it, they wouldn't be buying fur coats and capes, would they?"

"What are you, a college debater or something?"

"No ma'am," he says with a cute grin. "I know better than have traps without my name on them. This one might've slipped off or something."

"Nice try, Wayne. I'm issuing a citation for this trap and this instance. I need the mink you put in your pouch and will be taking this trap with me as evidence. You can check your other traps for compliance, before I stumble onto them or get another complaint."

Wayne's grin disappears as he reaches into his pouch for the mink. As he extends it to me he asks, "How do you know this is the mink I pulled from this trap? Don't you need to know, **this is the same animal from this trap**?"

"Hand over the mink, Wayne, and don't get wise." I take the small creature and look in its mouth. "Yep, this is the one." I hand the citation over, "Wayne, pay up the fine and

Kim Millick
Falmouth, ME

get your other traps in order. If you have any questions about the chain of evidence or whether you can get out of the citation, look here." I hold out the mink pointing to the earring placed in its mouth. "That's mine."

***

Laureen Haben, osf
Milwaukee, WI

A-Courting He Did Go

In his spring ritual
   the male spruce grouse postures to begin.

Feathered in black and white plumage
  with brow of red
   he spreads his fan
   to reveal brown tipped tail.

Parading his strut
  he listens for an eager mate.

Having attracted no one
   in but a few seconds
    he flaps his wings
     and flutters high to a limb

only to repeat his dance
  eight times in twenty minutes.

Sally Woolf-Wade
New Harbor, ME

Depending on the Tide

The tide, running out
sucks life from the day.
The sea lies still
silent and thoughtful
holds its breath so long
it appears to be dead.

But it revives, turns
as if undecided,
circles in eddies,
slowly rises once again.

Incoming tide swells,
smiles at the shore,
creeps to embrace
those of us on land
who wait gratefully
for its kiss.

***

Sylvia Little-Sweat
Wingate, NC

Granddaughter

Little Bumblebee—
swaddled in April flannel—
swill my heart's nectar.

John Kieran Henry
Shelton, CT

September Eleventh Two Thousand and One

September eleventh, two thousand and one
A day of infamy in our world

The sky was bright and blue
With nary a cloud in sight
The morning streets of New York were bright
While Washington was coming alive
In Pennsylvania all seemed serene
But soon it would become surreal.

September eleventh two thousand and one
Its memory will live forever
Each person who lived that terrible day
Remember precisely where they were
When cowards swooped from the sky
And claimed innocent lives
Evil men professing love of God
But their activities mirrored Satan

In a field in Pennsylvania
Some wicked men died,
Their names will be forgotten
They are of no importance
But on that fateful day
Many heroes were born
Spurned on by one man
Who cried aloud "Let's Go"

In Washington and New York
More despots from above
Took many noble lives

(continued)

John Kieran Henry
Shelton, CT

And destroyed so many buildings.
Citizens of New York City
Watched in horror as buildings fell
As deadly smoke enveloped streets
And people fell to death from above.

So many died on that fateful day
So many other lives were changed
Cities plunged into mourning
And a nation awakened to danger
Never again would we know innocence
After September eleventh, two thousand and one.

***

Mark D. Biehl
Hales Corners, WI

Leaves

Sentinels of snow
Leaving their summer home
Alone and in clustering swirls,
Drifting smoothly, gliding,
Slamming downward,
Wind snapped,
Gusting,
Lying still.

Green
Yellow orange
Magenta
Brown

Leaves

Jennifer Greenleaf
Topsham, ME

Rounds

Knocked down
Filled with fear
Doubts, confusion
With pain
I must get up
And test my strength
My convictions
My desire to be
More than he sees
More than they say
Judged on mistaken words
I hide my heart
My very being
Keep it safe
From those
Unwilling to see
Who I work to be
They are unworthy
So I stand tall
Gloves off the ropes
Knowing I must test
My heart against my enemy
My greatest foe
The darkest inhabitant
Of my soul

Myself

John Leggett
Falmouth, ME

The Canfield

My friends and I grew up in Aroostook County, Maine. Throughout the long winters we built snow forts or tramped through the woods. In spring we shagged fly balls, and during summer months we skinny-dipped in Mr. McKindley's pond. Fall was different. Fall brought on the three-week closing of school to allow for the back-breaking ritual of picking potatoes.

There were six of us—Arnie, James, Alan, the Levesque twins, and me. Arnie, at fifteen, was one year older than the rest of us; James was the defiant one and Alan the daredevil. The Levesque twins, Mark and Benjamin, were inseparable. Benjamin's decisions were made by Mark because Mark was seventeen minutes older; a fact he never hesitated mentioning. My talent was being the tallest.

At harvest time, we picked potatoes for Mr. Cyr and, of course, the number of barrels we filled became a competition. In October of 1958, however, a wedge was driven into our competitive midst . . . a wedge named Ida Oullette.

IT STARTED ON THE day prior to picking. We stopped by Mr. Cyr's farm on our way home from church. We always rode to the field in the back of his pickup truck and we needed to confirm his time of departure. While there, we were introduced to Ida. Actually, there was no introduction, Mr. Cyr simply pointed to her with the knife he'd just used to cut a plug of tobacco. She was sitting with her back against the barn dangling a piece of string just out of reach of a kitten. Even from a distance, Ida looked different—different from girls we knew. Her clothes and her hair . . . even the way she acted with the kitten seemed different. I thought I saw some orange nail polish on the hand holding the string.

"That fine young lady sittin' over there is my niece Ida,"

John Leggett
Falmouth, ME

he said. "She'll be workin' with you in the field this year."
We stood . . . speechless . . . not hiding our shock very well.
After trading horrified stares, James finally spoke. "Oh," he
said.

Benjamin scuffed his right foot back and forth in the dirt
causing serious damage to one of his Sunday shoes. We
would tolerate her of course. After all, she was Mr. Cyr's
niece. But didn't he realize we were six, not seven? There
was no room for seven in our outfit, and certainly not a
female seventh. I glanced at the Ida girl again. I knew she
heard her uncle's introduction but she never gave us one
speck of recognition. Not one speck.

"I'm counting on you boys to help her along—teach her
the ropes."

"Sure, we'll teach her everything she needs to know,"
Arnie lied, pretending we were pleased to have her.

"Ida lives in New York City," Mr. Cyr continued. "She'll
just be here for a month or so."

She stood, seemingly bored with kitten teasing, and then
Mr. Cyr's ten-year-old daughter, Katie, came out of the house
and she and Ida disappeared into the barn. *Not too friendly,*
I thought. *Not very respectful either, just walking away like
that. Didn't she know who we were?* I then heard an unfamil-
iar tapping coming from the barn. I was curious as to what
it was but, of course, showed no interest. It was the first time
I heard that tapping . . . but not the last.

ON THE WALK HOME we discussed our problem—the
pros and cons of Ida working with us. There were no pros of
course, and after considerable discussion, we agreed on
rules of engagement. It was decided no one was to initiate a
conversation with her and only short answers were to be
given if she had questions related to picking potatoes.
Anyone breaking the rules was to be excommunicated. The
decision was unanimous.

The next morning, we sat in the back of the truck waiting

John Leggett
Falmouth, ME

for Ida. The rhythmic tapping I'd heard the day before was again coming from the barn. It stopped when Mr. Cyr honked the horn and Ida and Katie came outside. Ida climbed into the truck's cab and Katie, being too young to pick, went into the house.

The first day was hard, especially for Ida. It was a long day of back-breaking work that none of us were used to. In the field, it was obvious she needed instruction. At first she stood and just stared at the ground. "So where am I supposed to dig up these stupid potatoes?" she finally asked.

Information about picking was allowable so I explained. "Bernie over there on the tractor is the jobber. He'll stake out a row for you and dig 'em up. He'll probably give you a short length to start out as you've never picked before. But you have to know which barrels to fill and put one of your cards in so you'll get paid what you're supposed to."

She stood with her hand looped through her basket handle which then came to rest on her hip. She contorted her mouth and rolled her eyes at my advice. I noticed her nail polish didn't look so good up close; it was cracked and peeling and by lunch time it was gone.

For several days I kept an eye on her. The first week was rough but she never uttered a complaint. I found Ida to be somewhat intriguing. Despite the no talking rule, I occasionally engaged in brief conversations. She talked about New York City and how it differed from The County.

She confessed she didn't get along with her mother which was the reason she was visiting her uncle; they both felt they needed what her mother referred to as a "cooling off" period. As the days wore on, the chip on her shoulder seemed to get smaller and in a strange way, we became friends. I liked hearing about life in the big city and, although Arnie and the others never actually talked to her, they leaned in and strained to hear what she had to say. Eventually, when they wanted specifics, our pact of "no talking first" dissipated. We were resigned to have Ida with us for the entire harvest and

John Leggett
Falmouth, ME

our group became seven.

ON FRIDAY OF THE first week, we broke for lunch and the conversation turned to The Canfield . . . a feat originated and performed a decade earlier by the legendary Jimmy Canfield. Jimmy was one of the few guys in high school who could dunk a basketball . . . a jumping ability that was further demonstrated when he entertained fellow pickers during harvest lunch breaks. He would put an empty barrel in a furrow, stand on the adjacent mound, and jump straight up in the air and come down inside it. Other pickers attempted it, but none had ever been successful.

I had heard of The Canfield but I never met anyone who actually witnessed it. Some believed Jimmy did it—others were skeptical. During every harvest, however, talk of The Canfield always surfaced and some fool had to try it. Attempts usually ended with the jumper discovering in mid air that he wasn't going to make it and, rather than risk the dangerous repercussions of a straddled landing, the attemptee kicked the side of the barrel and knocked it over. Farmers frowned upon the lunch-time antics for fear of broken bones or worse yet . . . broken barrels.

By the end of the second week, James, and a picker from an adjacent field, had attempted it. Being unsuccessful, they discussed new maneuvers that might increase their chance for success. Midway in their talk, an unfamiliar voice came from nowhere. "I could do it," said the voice. The statement came from Ida and held the calm conviction of assurance.

A pall followed . . . lingering birds stopped chirping . . . the chewing of peanut butter sandwiches were halted in mid-chews and Alan, who had just taken a large bite of an apple, stared at the white innards as if it was a crystal ball and was going to offer an explanation for the absurd comment.

"You?" James said. "You think you can do The Canfield?" The question held the potential for goading Ida into an embarrassing predicament of sure-fired failure. We waited

John Leggett
Falmouth, ME

like hunters in a blind, hoping she would take the bait.

"Yeah, I could do it. I mean, all you have to do is jump up in the air and come down inside the barrel right?"

"It's a little more complicated than that," James said, although it really wasn't. "Nobody's been able to do it in over uh, well, probably at least ten years! Your skinny little girlie legs sure aren't gonna do it!" None of us had actually seen Ida's legs, but we assumed they matched her skinny little arms.

Ida remained calm and brushed a few crumbs from her overalls. "Yeah, I think I can do it. In fact, I know I can do it."

"Yeah? Well maybe you should put your money where your mouth is." Bang! James had set the trap and she'd walked right into it. He continued, "I'll bet my entire three week's earnings you can't do no Canfield!"

A contemplative silence followed before Ida responded, "Well, I'd be willin' to bet half."

"Whaddaya mean half?"

"You know . . . half your earnings. I'd feel bad takin' *all* your money. Even from you James. In fact, I'll match half the pay of anybody who wants to bet."

"Where you gonna get that much money? You gotta have it to bet it," James warned.

"I've got money. I brought money with me . . . from New York," Ida lied. "Besides, I won't be losing any to you."

Alan dug his heel into the dirt. "I'll take some of that bet," he said without looking up. Benjamin looked at Mark who gave him a negative nod of his head and, for once, without any argument, the twins remained silent.

James looked at Arnie. "Don't go lookin' at me," Arnie said. "The whole idea is stupid."

It seemed everyone was waiting for my decision. I looked at Ida. She was staring off into the potato fields not giving any hint of what she was thinking.

"I think I'll sit this one out," I said.

"Okay," said James, "then we'll make you the official ref-

John Leggett
Falmouth, ME

eree. Anybody object to that?" The answer was a unified shrug. Ida said nothing.

"How 'bout it girlie? That okay with you?" James chided. For the first time, Ida looked directly at me. She held her gaze and then shot a glance back at James. "Agreed," she said.

One other rule," James added. "You can't tell your uncle about the bet." And then as an afterthought added, "or anybody else."

"Fine by me. I wouldn't want him to know I was takin' your money anyway."

"So, let's see you do it then," he told her. "Plenty of barrels sittin' around. Take your pick."

"Not today." Ida made the statement like she was bored with all of it.

"When then?"

"The last day of pickin'. That'll be payday anyway so I'll make sure I get my money."

James looked at me, presumably because I was the referee. "Her money, her call," I said with a shrug, and everyone seemed satisfied.

The days leading up to the wager held a different air than those in the previous weeks. Less joking except for jokes made at the expense of "skinny legs." But I never saw any sign of worry on Ida's face. She either believed she could do it or she was playing poker and had an ace up her sleeve.

On the day the moment of truth arrived Ida inspected the barrels. "I wanna get one without any nails sticking out of the rim," she said.

As referee, I accompanied her and when she settled on the one she wanted, I carried it near the spectators. Pickers from other fields wandered over. After all, there was some girl from New York City—attempting The Canfield—for money. There was no way news like that remained a secret.

Ida selected the mound from which she was going to jump. Mound height was the only clear advantage and she took her time. James examined the mound for any big rocks

John Leggett
Falmouth, ME

which might allow for a hard-surfaced advantage while I placed the barrel in the adjacent furrow. As referee, I pushed down on it to ensure its stability. Everything seemed satisfactory.

I then felt I needed to make a statement—give proper respect to the event—so I summoned up my best voice. "The feat known as *The Canfield* will now be attempted by Miss Ida . . . Miss Ida . . ." She gave me her customary skewed look and then finished her name. "Oullette!" she asserted.

"Oullette!" I repeated, realizing I never knew her last name. "To be successful, she must jump into the air and come down inside the barrel without tipping it over." The statement also acted as a disclaimer to eliminate any later arguments. Everything seemed ready.

A thick silence hovered over the field that day and no one, not even James, said a word. Ida removed her jacket and sweater and took her time walking to the mound. She turned and faced us but stared out at the gray horizon. It was a good ten or fifteen seconds before she made her move. The initial silence swelled into a cloud that seemed to hover over all of us and the significance of the moment became an historic reality.

Ida bent her knees ever so slowly and lowered herself by twelve to fourteen inches. Her back remained perfectly straight, as if she was a concert pianist sitting down to play. It seemed an eternity before her next move and then, without warning, she shot up like a dart. She seemed to hang there— the bottoms of her feet no more than an inch higher than the top of the barrel—and then her body floated down with the delicacy of a feather. She stood . . . inside the barrel—perfectly calm—perfectly erect—with her arms stretched outward to maintain her balance. She didn't smile or smirk. She just stood with that skewed-faced look I'd come to know. I can't recall ever witnessing anything so graceful. Ida Oullette had done The Canfield.

Spectators cheered and applauded. I was so flabbergast-

John Leggett
Falmouth, ME

ed that I forgot my role of referee. I finally stumbled to the barrel, took hold of Ida's wrist, and raised her arm straight up like a champion boxer. "I declare that Miss Ida Oullette has successfully completed the feat known as The Canfield."

Cheers and applause escalated in appreciation of her accomplishment. James and Alan looked at each other. James picked up a small rock and threw it into the dirt in disgust. I instinctively reached under Ida's arms to help her out of the barrel. As I lifted, she brought her knees to her chest and her lithe frame seemed to float upward. She then straightened her legs and stood before me and I found myself reluctant to release my grip.

The remainder of the day was quiet. After her accomplishment, Ida sat against the lone tree in the field and ate her lunch. She pulled a paperback from her coat and read until the end of the day. Mr. Cyr arrived and distributed our pay envelopes and, as the referee, I oversaw the reluctant payments made by James and Alan.

I DIDN'T SEE IDA during the week that followed, but on the day she was to leave, Mr. Cyr called and asked me to go along and help with her suitcase. I knew she didn't need any help but flattered myself by thinking it was her idea. When I arrived, that rhythmic tapping was coming from the barn again. This time I investigated. I found Katie inside twirling a jump rope. Her hand held one end of the rope with the other end tied to a post. Each revolution made a tapping sound as it hit the floor.

"Do you wanna jump?" Katie asked.

"Jump? No, I don't think so."

"I'm real good at twirling," she said. "I twirl for Ida every day. You should see *her* jump. She wins jump-roping contests and everything in New York. She's got trophies and everything."

"She does?" I responded. "Trophies?"

"Yeah, her legs are really strong. She won the *Single Jump* contest and the *Double Dutch* contest two years in a

John Leggett
Falmouth, ME

row. You should see her. The other day she stood on that box and jumped up in the air and came down right into that barrel over there!"

I stared at the barrel Katie was pointing to. "Did Ida ever talk about something called The Canfield?" I asked.

"The Canfield? No, what's a Canfield?"

"Never mind."

I left the barn and Ida came out and we climbed into the truck.

"Jump rope champion . . . trophies?" I asked.

Ida stared out the windshield. "Just practicin' for when I get home." And before the conversation continued, Mr. Cyr climbed in and we left for the bus depot. At the station, I performed my duty of carrying Ida's suitcase.

"You were a good referee," she said. "Are you going to tell them about my jumping?"

"Nothin' to tell. Nothin' says you're not allowed to practice."

"James and Alan may not agree with that," she said and we both laughed.

"Hey, maybe I'll come back next fall. Pickin' wasn't so bad ya know? And I sure am richer." As she made the comment she patted her wallet and we both laughed a second time.

When the bus pulled out I waved a good-bye through a smudged window. My assumption that she would never come back was correct. On the ride home, I thought about what she'd said about being richer and realized I was richer too.

Joann R. Hooper
Rockland, ME

Timely Seasons

In Maine, March and April, the awakening of Spring is slow
Gradually, because of the melting ice and snow.
Pussy willows and robins surprisingly appear
Dandelion, crocus and daffodils make their premier.
Geese arriving hearing their trumpet cries on going
Spears of green grass poking up and freely growing.
Trees looking alike with the rebirth of leaves budding out
Maple syrup running, Spring has arrived without any doubt.

As summer progresses with a green carpet on the lawn
And new arrivals of life in the early dawn.
Warm breezes and birds singing their song
Brings a happy outlook and inspiration along.
Enjoying summer with all the activities one can do
Parades, cookout, camping, swimming, paddling a canoe.
Hiking, boating, road trips and skies of blue
Beautiful scenery and healthy air to mention a few.

When the golden colors of Fall explode
Harvesting of fields, trees and gardens by the truckload.
Canning, country fairs and splitting of wood
Bundling up for the cold weather is the likelihood.
First comes the early light fluffy snow
Preparing everyone for a fall northeasterly blow.

Winter is long, but the warmth from a stove fire
Brings forth happy memories and moments to inspire.
Snow activities bring joy and happiness to the young at heart
Long icicles looking like exquisite chandeliers glistening as
        works of art.
Frozen drops of water on a wire fence, look like diamonds in

(continued)

Joann R. Hooper
Rockland, ME

the sun
Lacy frost patterns on windows that nature has spun.
Looking back on the seasons of Spring, Summer, Fall and
        Winter transitions
Maine's unique evergreen pines and fir trees complete the
        composition.

***

Elmae Passineau
Weston, WI

Into the Night

Lightning slithered across the southern sky
    reaching for the tallest treetops
Thunder growled ominously
    low and distant
Raindrops, plump as gumdrops,
    plopped onto the picnic table—
    here, there, three, four,
    sparse enough to count
    but harbingers of what was coming

We ran for Grandma's and Grandpa's
    big black umbrellas,
    curled our skinny ten-year-old selves
    into the cushioned Adirondacks—
    Dad brought us blankets—

Warm and dry,
    giggles masking our fright,
    we watched the storm pass
    into the night

Carol Leavitt Altieri
Madison, CT

Trees in the Winter Forest

"When I say, '1Trees suckle their children,'
Everyone knows immediately what I mean."

I
The dynamic winter trees
fan their limbs over all, want to be watched,
and listened to. Standing trunk to trunk,
side by side, they protect their neighbors,
with choiring branches that allow the light
to touch all, not blocking other's light.
Admire their crowns against purplish-blue skies.

Inscribing touchstones,
some toss their hair, cut or colored leaves
changing and falling off. They fix wrinkled bark
like humans remaining similar through time.

II
The trees in my forest communicate with neighbors
and discover secrets from their world.
They can count and remember,
nurse neighbors, send electric signals
of danger across fungal networks
and keep other stumps alive.

Deep green moss and lichen grow on their barks,
make flesh, make food, make flowers.
In the winter quietness of the woodlands,
guarded by these stalwart sentinels,
roots intertwine under snow tracks of deer.
And a white-footed mouse loses its life

(continued)

Carol Leavitt Altieri
Madison, CT

in the drama of an owl's dinner.
In some level of sun, earth and water, we
are of the same rhythms dropping wealth
as seasons roll by—investing in the long view.

***

Roselyn Stewart
Brookfield, WI

October's End

On the horizon
Clouds thread past
A luminous moon

A black cat arches her
Back and hisses at a
Vaporous mist rising
Above a grave stone

A cauldron burps and
bubbles as a witch brews
a mysterious potion

Jack-o-lanterns
With toothy grins
Grimace from the dark

Frightened children
Tell ghost stories
around a fire

What mischief will this
Halloween bring

Eileen Hugo
Spruce Head, ME & Stoneham, MA

To Brave the Blackness

Bright full moon reveals the cave
a black wet hole on the bottom of the bluff.
Water washes in and out on the tide
the cave gulps rough.

Turmoil at the caves gaping door
draws us as close as we dare.
The sand slips out from under our feet
seaweed like flowing hair.

When low tide cycles back out from shore
approaching the cave with slow cautious stride.
Inside darker than a cold cloudless night
haunting noises from dark arise.

Could pirates have hidden booty there?
or sea monsters or giant squids awaiting a raid.
We pondered and decided not to go inside
admittedly afraid.

Dwayne Magee
Mechanicsburg, PA

Leaves

The most difficult of circumstances Elwood Palmer ever had to weather were those surrounding the death of his wife. Over a period of months he descended emotionally into a dull, hopeless existence. The only thing he could find the strength or will to believe in was the belief that he too would one day soon be dead. He was the last leaf on an otherwise barren tree. His tears were a cold, late autumn rain. He ate nothing. The color of life had faded from him until all that was left was a withered ghost. He waited for the wind to free him.

A year has passed since then. His life is very different now. Yes, the memories of those days still cling to him or perhaps he simply refuses to let them go, but they no longer define him.

The seasons have changed. Days have gone by. People have come and people have gone. The path that led her from him was somewhere in the past. It was deep in the hills of a distant place. He had only pretended to die with her.

Now, driving north to the cabin where he had stayed those first few months was bringing back a flood of emotion. Through the rearview mirror of his forest green pickup truck, he watched clusters of dead leaves drift down the road behind him. It was as if the leaves sensed themselves disintegrating. They were fleeing from their certain fate of decay and escaping desperately to some unknown place. They seemed full of regret.

"I know what it feels like to be those leaves," he uttered to himself.

The day seemed to pass by slowly as he traveled northward and the silence in his truck was sending him into an excessive state of self-contemplation. The trees were passing by him almost rhythmically and the whoosh sound they

Dwayne Magee
Mechanicsburg, PA

made was hypnotizing. He made a mental note to himself—
Fix the damn radio!

At long last, fingers of late afternoon sun light began
piercing through the dense forest around him and he knew
he was getting closer. He knew the road opened and became
wider in the last few miles. He was near the water now. With
the window down, he could smell it. He watched and listened
for the birds. He remembered watching birds when he
stayed here. On any given day he saw ducks, geese, ospreys,
eagles, hawks, loons, and herons. The cabin was often fre-
quented by another of nature's wonders, the double rainbow.
It was as if God himself was hiding here.

The river by the cabin was part of one of the oldest river
systems in the world. It was older than the mountains
through which it ran. Its waters were life giving and they pro-
vided a home to a wide variety of living things, not just the
birds. The breathtaking scenery of rural New England was
spectacular and for Elwood, it was healing. He could not
think of a better place to say goodbye.

He parked the truck in a clearing above the river.

The wooden urn felt light in his aged hands.

"Good bye Laurel," he whispered.

And he gave up her ashes to the wind.

Irene Zimmerman
Greenfield, WI

Autumn Afternoon at Rosie's Corner

The long valley yawns before us,
spreading wide its quilted yellow,
green, gold and ochre fields
of hay, beans and corn.

We sit in stillness listening to
our squeaking swing,
the rustle of drying corn nearby,
a hawk's cry as it rides a thermal.

Everything around us whispers *shhhh.*
And then we hear the breath of God
bringing forth the world.

***

On the Cusp of Spring

The maple trees have shed their snowy clothes,
and now the sap is hurrying to dress
their trunks in green. Along the woodchip trail,
the sun curdles old snow, collecting
whey in shallow bowls. A Canada goose
lands, skids, crashes through the pond's
thin ice to make a goose-wide swimming hole.
Repeatedly, it coils its gooseneck down
and up, sipping spring champagne, then waddles
awkwardly toward shore, shattering
the pond's porcelain lid with every step.

Dawn Edwards
Ipswich, MA

10

I gracefully run along the pristine shoreline
breathing in ocean air, reveling in knowing
my physique and flowing blond locks are admired.
I am perfect.

I greet my guests in a slinky Calvin Klein design.
They delight in my carefully prepared escargot
and rave over my elegant Saumon Val DeLoire.
I am perfect.

I'm told I have a designer's flair in my home.
The custom rug in golden hues complements
two antique chairs on either side of the fireplace.
I am perfect.

I believe I'm flawless in every way, accepted by all
and have no doubts about getting into heaven.
After all, Jesus said, "Be ye therefore perfect."
I am perfect.

But wait, I'm told perfect means whole and complete,
that Jesus did not mean we're not allowed mistakes.
I cover my secret, insecure feelings by saying
I am perfect.

So now I'm beginning to sense my "self," to know
myself as part of the whole of creation.
I gratefully surrender the need to be perfect.
I'm free.

Patricia T. Graves
York, ME

Ageless: Despite Evidence to the Contrary

When Addy settled in at her favorite desk, the one with the chiseled heart in the upper right corner, she forgot how old she was. Even though she knew nothing about their lives, she felt a camaraderie with the hot-shot ivy-leaguers hunched over nearby desks and tables—a shared earnestness for discovery, for learning, for creative endeavor. The rapid tapping of their fingers on keyboards echoed her own rhythmic typing; the LED backlighting of their PC's reflected in her own screen—mingling with the display of her novel's next page. Unlike many her age, Addy had made it her business to learn how to use a computer—one of those lightweight laptops that didn't aggravate her arthritic neck when she slipped it into the cushioned bag and hefted it onto her shoulder.

Swaddled in the glow of the green-shaded lamp, cradled by the hushed surroundings; she surrendered and gave her muse permission to write without her interference. With every stroke across the keys, she anticipated the surprises that would appear before her in twenty-five point font—the twists of phrase, the metaphors comparing entities whose similarities she'd not recognized before and, best of all, the completely unforeseen O'Henry endings.

While it was true that on the inside she felt ageless, she was well aware that on the outside no one would mistake her for a co-ed. She wasn't, after all, so desperate to fit in that she'd shed her cable-knit sweaters and relaxed-fit jeans for tops that plunged dangerously close to the navel and leggings that accentuated every ripple. She preferred to keep her anatomy to herself—thank you very much. And just in case her attire wasn't enough of a give-away, there were the veined hands, the crisply-cut white hair and the thick-lensed spectacles punctuating the fact that nature was having its

Patricia T. Graves
York, ME

way with her.

She'd learned early on that not every student who passed between the Corinthian columns and through the arched doorway was ablaze with creative spark. Originally she made her library treks in the afternoons. The loudly-whispered discourse about who'd been kicked off some island and who'd hooked up with whom, coupled with the ever-present buzz of vibrating phones, literally drove her to distraction. She was on the cusp of abandoning her forays amongst the stacks when Addy heard on the radio that the main library would now be open twenty-four hours a day. From that point on she napped in the afternoon and waited until midnight to slide into the Windsor desk chair by the third Palladian window.

At that hour, only those committed to serious work were present—usually with their cell phones fast asleep in their pockets. The industriousness of these scholars energized her. Her short stories became a novella; her novella a four hundred-page novel. In fact the spell of her muse was so compelling that she'd had to be careful not to lose track of time. It was critical that she head the Buick toward home no later than five AM while the roads were still empty. The last thing she needed was some antsy driver honking at her for going twenty miles an hour or a hot-headed adolescent hollering obscenities when her high beams poured through his windshield.

Tonight, she'd left her computer at home atop a stack of packing crates. She suspected this would be her last visit so she'd come to say good-bye, to imprint the library's essence on her memory. She inhaled the faintly musty smell of aging books, ran her hand along the varnished window sill and scrutinized with a magnifying glass the desktop initials to clarify if it was Dan or Don who was enamored with Mary—silently sending them a wish that their love would be as enduring as her own passions had been.

For years her children had nattered on about how they

Patricia T. Graves
York, ME

were too worried about her going out alone at night to allow her trips to the library to continue. Didn't she know that old ladies were prime targets for muggers and even rapists, believe it or not? It was time, they insisted, for her to live somewhere safer and closer to them so they could keep an eye out. These lectures began when she turned eighty and she'd held out for nearly ten years—dismissing their pleas as melodramatic and hyperbolic. She reminded them that the motion-sensitive spotlight her son rigged up on the garage was quite successful in depriving her of all privacy as she exited and entered her home, and the library parking lot was nearly as bright as Fenway during a night game. No, she was most confident that no self-respecting mugger or rapist was about to attack a fully-illuminated wobbly old woman.

Then a few days before her ninetieth birthday, her daughter, Olivia, walked in while a graduate student was reading Addy's manuscript out loud then editing it per Addy's oral instructions. There was no more hiding it—in spite of the consumption of mounds of leafy vegetables and the scrupulous use of sun glasses, the breakdown of her maculae was progressing in both eyes. She could no longer do her own proofreading, and it was clear that she would not be passing the upcoming driver's exam. No license, no library, no more holding out.

Satisfied Dan, not Don, was Mary's beau; Addy slipped the magnifying glass into her purse, felt for the chain along the side of the lamp and tugged out the light. With both hands pressed against the desktop, she hoisted herself up, steadied her fickle legs, and with a nod to Emily at the circu-lation desk, walked slowly and regally toward the double doors. Outside, Olivia waited for her in the Buick.

Barbara Ryland
South Portland, ME

Red

Merlot, Sangria, and Pinot Noir flowed through our laughter
        and chatter
that year in Europe. Tables dressed in white linens. Vases
        of red
roses in the center of each seemed to watch us in delight.
In the background a guitarist played Gypsy music. Its beats
        strummed through our blood
and rushed to our faces flushing them rouge.
Onion, garlic, and tomato scents wafted through the air,
        turning our salivary glands to water.
We were so in love then.

But that was before I carried our daughter in my womb.
That was before the hemorrhage that burst from my body, a
        sudden river of red running over
                furniture and floors bearing her away even as
                our love ebbed.

And now, years later, the rosebush by my backdoor,
        watered with love and memory,
offers deep red buds, petals unfurling, opening in the sun.

Robert Witte
Waldoboro, ME

Evening Anchorage

We sailed out of Camden on the *Nonsuch*
That bright afternoon,
Southeast until we cleared the ledges.
Then Gordon put her head round, and we bore away
To the east'ard. The wind began to blow through my body.
"Keep her headed so while I trim the sails."

Between Job's and the Ensigns we tacked her
To the north'ard, then wing and wing up Gilkey Harbor,
(Wind streaming through my mind and ribs now)
Past Seven Hundred Acre, Thrum Cap, and around the
          corner.
Rounded into the southerly breeze, dropped our hook.
(Right between Spruce and Warren.)

"My, its pretty here!" "Yeah, nice and snug.
You got supper ready yet?"
In the tawny evening light, little sloops rocked
Like sleepy ducks, and we drank a toast to the three of us.
Ate supper, played guitar, drank another toast.
Later, put out another anchor, more for the hell of it
Than need.

Morning come, with a flat-arse calm; some fish crows
Working the edge between the woods and shore.
We headed back in later, under power.
"She's not got enough keel to claw up to windward."
I guess there were things that needed doing.
No time to waste sailing her in, was there?

Karyn Lie-Nielsen
Waldoboro, ME

Arrhythmia

My heart was doing the tango
or maybe it was the mamba.
Mallets running percussive
scales on wooden bars.
A coronet in the background.

My heart was reading too many suspense novels.
Traveling in exotic places
tracking down some spy ring
in Brazil or maybe it was Istanbul.
A frantic chase, gunshots in the alley.

My heart was careening
the steep hills of San Francisco
in a hopped-up old Chevy Malibu
pounding hard on blacktop
at the crest of each blind hill.
My heart was running red lights
dodging little old women out walking
their dogs or maybe it was baby carriages
and hot-dog stands,
sirens shrieking a hair's breadth behind.

That's how my heart was.
Falling out of sync
doors swinging open
slamming shut willy-nilly push and pump here and there
a manic rush to catch up.

There I was, a little dizzy in the flower beds
standing in good rubber boots alone with my heart.

(continued)

Goose River Anthology, 2016//98

Karyn Lie-Nielsen
Waldoboro, ME

Or maybe I was doing a small waltz,
raking cordate leaves from a nearby birch,
when my heart, like a wild pony, spooked
at the specter of death in the browning garden,
the terrifying news about stopping, now,
in the middle of a dance.

***

Delphiniums

rise.
The June sky
   does nothing to discourage such blue
   passionate fortitude.
      Tall proud stalks seduce even the sun.

Spikes
of starlike
   flowers: Magic Fountains, Galahad,
   centered "bees," just a dab
      of color, no sting, handsome Black Knight.

Flounced
and bouncing
   peonies, forever aground, can't
   rival the slim reach, pro-
      found elegance of delphiniums.

Then
jealous wind
   takes them or the calendar page turns
   and empty spaces learn
      how nature, unkind, favors nothing.

Goose River Anthology, 2016//99

David Campbell
Somerville, MA

Rembrandt Self-Portrait
for Richard Maury

Old man, the late man, his flesh load
a superfluity not to be glossed over.
Life does not so much take back

its gifts, its cap of feathers,
its promise and praise,
as mock them before his eyes.

Ungifted, unpromising pupils
fall from him like leaves
to curl back into the soil.

His wives are banked-up fires
around him in the gloom. Just paint,
they might give warmth for ages.

Each man the Atlas
of his own worldly skull.
The strength comes from...

What comes—passivity,
this habit-forming looking glass?
A waste, these thoughts

that darken daylight.
The visual is everything,
or else why paint?

Scott Carty
Peoria, AZ

He Made a Difference

The year was 1969. Fall was in the air and Issaquah High School, nestled in the foothills of the "Issaquah Alps," was a tranquil scene of quiet remoteness. Each school day began the same, with many students "hanging around" in the SAC, (Student Activity Center). Vietnam was a major concern to many seniors on campus and occasionally a heated debate about our role "over there" could be heard in the SAC. I was only a sophomore and while I was aware of the war, from TV and newspapers, it was only a minor blimp on my radar screen of daily activities. Life was good. I was on the wrestling team, had a job at the local candy store, lived on Lake Sammamish and hunting season was just around the corner.

My first quarter classes were not difficult. A medium amount of effort equated to "A"s and "B"s on my report card in all my classes except one. I was getting a "D" in World History. This of course did not fit into my "life was good" world. A "D" simply was unacceptable and I wasn't going to allow one teacher to screw up my otherwise rosy report card.

I made an appointment to talk to this teacher and get this "D" thing settled. In my mind it was a simple mistake on the teacher's part, and once I explained where I was coming from, he would gladly revise the grade to a more acceptable "B". I wasn't going to push it. I just wanted what was duly mine. I mean, I did the homework, sat in his classes, asked questions, was attentive, and behaved like a good student should. What more could a teacher want. Besides it worked in my other classes well enough.

So one day after school I sat down with my problem teacher and after a few words about the weather, I expressed myself in plain English how wrong he was to give me a "D". In my mind I was very persuasive and was sure I was scoring

Scott Carty
Peoria, AZ

some major points. He simply sat there behind his desk, a small smile on his face, gently taping his fingers together. I finished on a high note saying I enjoyed his class and with that sat back pretty darn proud of myself.

"Scott, you're skating," came slowly from his lips. His eyes locked onto mine and the smile disappeared. "The 'D' stands."

I was shell-shocked. My stomach felt like someone sucker punched me. I was speechless. My mouth opened and closed half a dozen times before I was able to utter "What?"

My mind was racing, trying to find an alternative approach. It was obvious he didn't "buy" my first attempt. I was down, but not out. This could still be salvaged; I just needed to attack from a different angle.

I explained how busy my schedule was, what with my job and all, and being on the wrestling team and being on the student council. It was a good approach, had some merit and was basically the truth. *Score another one*, I thought.

He held up his hand and said, "Scott, you are not working to your potential. You're dogging it and your effort is worth a 'D'."

His words were spoken firmly and evenly. Each word hit me hard. I felt real pain. I could not believe this SOB had the gall to actually say what he did. Gradually my disbelief turned into anger. I could feel my face getting hot, and for the first time in my life I understood how powerful an emotion hate was. In the back of my mind, hidden yet accessible, was the thought that I would actually enjoy hurting this person. I knew better than to act on that thought, but it scared me that I could even think it.

He continued, "When you give me 'A' effort, I'll give you an 'A'."

I picked up my books and left his class without saying another word. I was furious. It was a Friday and his words boiled inside me all weekend. By Sunday evening my folks

Scott Carty
Peoria, AZ

thought this teacher was none other than the devil himself, come to earth to make my life a living hell. They listened to my ranting and raving, nodded their heads with parental understanding and basically said nothing. Finally just before I went to bed that Sunday evening, my dad said, "Scott, forget about the 'D', it's only a letter, do yourself a favor and listen to what he's saying."

Great Dad, easy for you to say, you don't have to sit in this guy's class everyday. I was still too emotionally attached to my position, my self image to see anything but my view on the subject.

In his class I basically became a non-entity. I was going through the motions, but I figured, *Hey, I'm getting a 'D', why waste any effort on this dude.* Over the next few weeks, it was obvious to everyone but myself that my attitude was affecting not only my schoolwork but other aspects of my life as well. I was in classic denial and still upset with how unfair he was to me.

Finally the end of the quarter came and I figured, *Okay, he made his point, he sees how down I am and he'll give me at least a 'C' for showing up.* Now, that took some effort! I could not believe it when I saw a "D-" on my report card. To say I went ballistic was an understatement.

I ran into his class and threw my report card on his desk and nearly yelled, "What is the meaning of this? You gave me a 'D-'."

He got up from his desk, asked the remaining kids in the room to leave and then shut the door. Outside, it was raining, the wind was blowing hard and the air was biting cold and my mood was just as ugly as the weather.

I sat in the chair next to his desk ready to pounce on anything he had to say. I was mad and he was going to pay. There is nothing more righteous than justified anger.

He sat down behind his desk and looked at me for the longest time and finally said, "You and I have a problem."

Scott Carty
Peoria, AZ

The guy's a genius, I thought to myself.

"We obviously share different views of your capabilities. I find you to be a very intelligent, inquisitive individual who enjoys life. You on the other hand must see yourself as something less."

Whoa! I thought I was ready for anything, but he was coming from a different planet. I sat there, stunned, trying not to look too shocked.

"My rules are straight forward, I've been honest with you from day one and you still believe that I'm going to change my rules just because you don't happen to agree with them."

Somehow I felt the righteous anger turning slowly to embarrassment. I was still mad, but I was beginning to squirm ever so slowly.

We sat in silence for a few moments looking at each other. Sizing up the situation as it were. I was not prepared for what he said next.

"Scott, I'll make a deal with you. If you give me your word that you'll give 100% effort in my class for the next quarter, I'll give you an 'A' for the year."

Suddenly the world looked brighter, I could see a way out of this hole, and it wasn't going to cost me anything. For an "A" I could easily work a little harder in his class and come out smelling like a rose.

I stood up with a smile on my face and said, "You've got a deal." I picked up my report card from his desk, grabbed my books and shook his hand. I made my way to the door feeling like a ton of bricks had suddenly melted off of my shoulders. My world was near perfect again.

Just as I was about to leave he said seven words that I shall never forget.

"Scott, remember you gave me your word!"

Those seven words hit me with such an impact that I still get teary eyed when I think of that moment. As I stood in the doorway, impervious to the cold wind, I could feel myself tee-

Scott Carty
Peoria, AZ

tering on the brink of manhood. Somehow we both knew that this was one of those precious moments in a person's life when a choice had to be made. A choice that would change forever how a life is lived.

I slowly turned to my teacher and said with a heavy voice, "Yes, I did."

I can't explain the emotions that were erupting inside me at that time. I wanted to cry, I wanted to dance. It was strange, yet wonderful at the same time. I felt an energy that I've rarely felt since, I not only gave 100%, I gave 110%. If there was one extra credit assignment, I would do two or three. He couldn't feed me fast enough, I was hungry for knowledge and I wanted desperately to please him, to prove to him that my word meant something.

True to his word he did give me the "A" for the year. But I was well past the token of the letter grade. I understood what it meant to extend yourself, to reach beyond your comfort zone, to rise to the challenge.

For the next three years of my high school career I took every class he offered. I got straight "A"s in everyone one of them and worked my butt off. He never wavered on his rules. I'm sure he would have given me a "D" if I deserved it.

We became good friends. We would sit for hours after school and discuss life in general and what was happening in the world at the time. Even after graduation, I would find time to drop in and visit for awhile. As time went on we saw less and less of each other, yet rarely a day goes by that I don't think of PJ and what a huge influence he had on my life.

Mr. Paul Victor Johnson gave me something that will remain with me to the day I die, he gave me the chance to become a man.

Patricia Lynne Janke
Wauwatosa, WI

Snippets

Sometimes precious memories
trickle from eyes as tears
Snippets flashing so vividly clear
Apparitions of past appear

Reach out touch the images
embracing this scene so vintage
are they real, are they alive
parading lightly through the mind?

Sensing laughter from beating hearts
an inner smile settles for a time
sipping luscious red wine
feeling the waves of ocean's tide

With closed eyes, hang on tight
to memories using all your might
not wanting to return to life
rejecting reality, You try to fight

If only one could remain here
a safe haven from all fear
of forgetting every year
and the loved ones held dear

Edie Schmoll
Menifee, CA

Never to See Again...

now that your eyes have been taken,
forever—
no more to see the sun shine
or the flowers;
to take joy in a rainbow
or bright morning hours;

the moonlight brings me sadness,
memories—
of looks of tender silence;
no more
sunsets, waterfalls, nature aglow,
for you—nothing but gray;

all the scenes you loved,
but I never did—
you were my day and my night;
and now that such joys are lost to you
forever,
I resent every lovely sight.

***

Sylvia Little-Sweat
Wingate, NC

Inkwell

You are the inkwell
I drink from at night to write—
the parchment, my heart.

Goose River Anthology, 2016//107

Marilyn Fleming
Pewaukee, WI

Six Tanka

a strangeness
in the foothills howling
at the moon
one more sleepless night
my mouth speaks wild sounds

First published in *Cattails,* September 2015

splitting wood
in-between the silence
flicker drums
in the palm of my hand
I cup your beating heart

First published in *Whispers in the Wind,* November 2015

feathers wild
pouring dust on their heads—
for a moment
a pottery artist
throwing clay on the wheel

First published in *Gogoyshi #3,* 2015

Marilyn Fleming
Pewaukee, WI

pipe in my mouth
watching a feather fall—
call of a macaw
into purple darkness
I step out of my skin

First published in *Gogoyshi #3,* 2015

quail nesting
in tall prairie grass
head tucked under wing—
I throw open my arms
and lift you to my hip

First published in *Blithe Spirit 26.1,* 2016

old carrots
the last of the root cellar
at first light
overwintered, bearded
I leave my cloistered cell

First published in *Skylark 4:1,* 2016

***

Sylvia Little-Sweat
Wingate, NC

Chambers

Like the nautilus
souls—sequestered—dive the Deep,
rest beneath the reef.

Jon Potter
Rockport, ME

Bookcase

Voices folded and tightly bound,
Shelved hard against each other—
Silent.
Glances pull memories of voices
Whispered tales of human growth,
Gritty spikes of tragedy,
Blankets of love.
Poets quietly exploding,
Chanting pictures which grip us hard,
Stab us with new thoughts.
The quiet voices
Together make a hushed murmur
Like the whisper of waves
Dissolving into a sand-filled beach.

***

P. C. Moorehead
North Lake, WI

Water Rising

The pain rises in me like a river,
overflowing the banks,
taking the trees,
invading my house.

I slam the windows,
grab the pillows,
hug to myself,
my comfort.

The river recedes.

Judith Andersen
Owls Head, ME

Oh, Syria

At a Forum on Foreign Relations meeting, we heard a speaker talk of his country, Syria, in glowing terms. Syria was ready for tourists; it had incredible antiquities, boutique hotels fashioned from old stately homes, a sophisticated cuisine, bustling souks, beautiful mosques, and even ATMs. We read a very positive article about the English-born Mrs. Assad in Vanity Fair, in which the chic and stylish First Lady was described as "The Desert Rose." All of this percolated in our subconscious for a few weeks, leading to an internet search for tourist information. Eureka! A small British company could set up a tour. We called, and before we could catch our breath, had a tour set up with a guide and driver for us in the Spring of 2011.

The Arab Spring had begun and scattered protests had started in Syria in February as I struggled to learn some basic Arabic, enough to be polite. We checked repeatedly with our travel agent and a well known expert on Syria. "Things should be okay," they said initially. We relaxed, then panicked, then cooled, then became restless again. A last phone call to the pundit was unsettling; he said he did not know what to expect. We started the trip nervously, reasoning that we could always leave, if necessary.

We stopped in London on the way, where on a walk, we wandered into Soho Square and encountered a dominating statue of St. Paul, struggling to hold his horse's reins as he was struck by his vision on the way to Damascus. This seemed an omen; we had to go on. Our very polite English relatives inquired, oh so kindly—as one would speak to the mad—whether we felt safe traveling to Syria. We reminded them that a huge, possibly violent demonstration was planned for Piccadilly the day after we left London. We learned a day later that the London riot had been violent.

Judith Andersen
Owls Head, ME

Even Fortnum and Mason's had been taken over.

On the flight to Damascus, we chatted with a mild-mannered physician who worked in London, but was returning to Latakia, to his wife and children he said, for a vacation. Though he expressed no worries, we noticed that he raced ahead of the line of people having baggage x-rayed, threw his case in the machine ahead of everyone else and raced out.

Our guide Sharif was there to greet us, as promised. He was a short fellow with kind brown eyes, a mustache, and a slight potbelly. My husband shook his hand, but I could not by custom, strange for someone in a culture in which a hug is a sign of casual friendliness. He warned us that there would be heavy traffic into Damascus due to a massive and chaotic pro-Assad demonstration. The palm-lined highway was a mosaic of erratically driven cars which made driving in Boston seem positively serene. My husband described it as motorized ballet gone amok. Every car had a Syrian flag hanging out the window. Decals of Bashar al Assad, Bashar with his father, Bashar with his children, covered rear car windows. Motorbikes sped by with whole families clinging on. Veiled mothers and their children were packed into the back of Toyota trucks, all waving flags in the spirit of the 4th of July. Horns honked and people shouted all the way into the old city. Even our van had a Syrian flag on the dash. We later saw a report on international television that showed clips of the demonstration we had witnessed, strangely calling it an anti-government rally.

When we finally arrived at our hotel, we found an exotically renovated home with a covered courtyard, a fountain and a songbird who was to be our alarm clock in a cage outside our room. The furniture was typically Syrian—dark wood with intricate inlays of shell. The young man who served us breakfast of bread, yoghurt and rolls, told us he had a cousin in Detroit. He, however, planned to stay in Syria and had a dream of starting a night club. He was wistfully young and sweet and hopeful.

Judith Andersen
Owls Head, ME

The Street Called Straight was close to our hotel. At either end of the long street were Roman ruins and as we ate snacks from a road stand, we perched on the remains of Roman columns in a small park. This quarter was surrounded by the walls which St. Paul traversed in a basket to escape his tormentors. The home of Ananias, where Paul was taken after his vision, remained as a chapel. Many inhabitants of the quarter were Christian. On our first day there we heard singing across the street, a song I remembered from the many crownings of the virgin as a child. In the courtyard of the Maronite Catholic Church a large group of young people were stepping to the rhythm of a booming drum, practicing for an Easter procession. On the outside wall of our hotel was a small shrine to Mary, under an Assad poster.

The Umayyad Mosque, which has since been bombed, was impressive with its foundation of Roman temple ruins and remains of a Christian church. The walls in the courtyard had elegant paintings of Paradise. The head of John the Baptist was reputably in one fenced-in shrine within the mosque, though there seem to be other heads in other mosques. Children played on the carpeted floor. Gaggles of women in black chadors with a slight white bill covering any stray hairs that would have peeked out walked in large groups with children and bearded men in white turbans, following leaders who carried red banners. As I walked in the courtyard of the mosque, covered in a brown hooded cloak of the visitor, walking in bare feet, I heard a rough voice shouting; "Where you from?" I answered in Arabic, and he seemed confused until his small daughter told him "America." He seemed shocked. Our guide explained that such groups were Iranian pilgrims and that very few Americans were seen in Syria.

We were taken to Naranj, a famous restaurant in the old city. Elegant young men, whose faces I had seen before in Babylonian friezes, were dressed in spotless tunics with white caps. They glided between tables carrying large trays of

Judith Andersen
Owls Head, ME

fruits and sweets, fragrant dishes of lamb and rice. The diners were relaxed, some finishing their meals by smoking their water pipes.

We traveled to many historic sites, but some stand in our minds and remain in our dreams. The Dead Cities were remnants of the Byzantine Fourth Century. The ruins included an intact Roman tavern; cows and chickens roamed peacefully through the dreamy abandoned town. Wildflowers dotted the landscape.

We reached our hotel in Aleppo after walking down a narrow cobblestone walk bordered by bakeries, metalwork shops, private homes, small markets. School children skipped by, holding hands. The front doors of the hotel were of polished brass and the interior glorious with multiple fountains and pools, sumptuous seating areas with jewel colored silk pillows, beams painted with flowers. Sitting on the roof, we looked on the citadel, a fortress and site of recent exciting Roman archaeologic digs by the French.

As we walked around the citadel one evening a young man called after us; he said he was the only Jew in Aleppo and was a silversmith whose family was in Italy now. He had come back as he saw a good future in Syria now. He took us through the Souk, the most impressive in the country, filled with everything from brassieres sold by men, toilet paper, candies, jewelry, antique paintings, camel hair clothing (soft as cashmere), household items, and it went on and on, building after building. Pungent spices in one hall scented the air, lending a mysterious oriental slant to the place.

On our last night in Aleppo we had dinner in an Armenian quarter and parked alongside a small square. When we returned the van had been booted. While our driver Nour looked for a policeman to pay, we watched a Baath party gathering in the square. Participants sat on fold-up metal seats and a leader half-sang and half-chanted loud flattering songs about Assad. People joined in periodically in the style of Southern tent revivals.

Judith Andersen
Owls Head, ME

Magical Palmyra, the ancient city in the desert, was akin to a mirage. A mile-long avenue filled with camels and their drivers was lined by tall Roman columns, and the road ended at the temple of Baal. A citadel stood overlooking the city on a hill; it still had bullet holes from the time of French Occupation. We arrived there at a new but almost deserted hotel on the edge of the ancient town, and saw no other occupants. At sunset a charming young Bedouin served us dinner on the front patio, bringing an enormous bread which he hung over his arm. The boy, for he was just a boy, spoke movingly about his love for the desert, the closeness of family, the code of courtesy to be followed for all visitors. The Bedouin bread which he had baked for us was offered in that spirit. Orange pillars and gateways, the Temple of Baal were otherworldly in the setting sun, transporting us back two thousand years. As we talked and looked out, we felt part of a dreamworld. There was a small but lovely museum of priceless treasure to see as well as Byzantine tombs dotting the hills.

The next morning CNN announced news that the United States warned Americans to leave the country. We had continued to wake up to conflicting news reports on television. Somehow our reservations evaporated each morning when we met up with our rock solid guide. But this morning, Shariff and Nour, after our normal discussion about sleep and the day ahead, both broke out in big smiles; they had been afraid we would ask them to take us to the airport, and were relieved that we had hung on. We took a circuitous path back to Damascus, stopped twice by men with guns who spoke only to the driver and our nervous guide, asking them for their identification. Our van was happily marked as tourist with official looking logo, unlike others we had seen with names like "Happy Trails," "Happy Journey," and "Honeymoon." We passed fields of airplanes covered by beige roofed shelters. We stopped at a popular cafe in the desert, The Baghdad Cafe, where one sat outside on well used camel

Judith Andersen
Owls Head, ME

saddles to drink tea and eat bread and cheese. Incongruously, it had the only flush toilet we saw in any rural area.

The Damascus to which we returned was sleepy on a weekend routine The markets were full. We strolled through the park beneath our western hotel, watching fathers pushing children on swings, women gossiping and eating snacks from a vendor, families happily picnicking on the grass. But the headlines on CNN told of riots throughout the country. In a day, we were gone, flying home, leaving with mixed feelings.

Tourism dwindled during our stay. There were groups early on from Germany, Italy, France and England. The English, mostly elderly, were intrepid, clambering over dangerously steep ruins, armed with walking sticks. Obviously a spot of war would not deter them. There had previously been large groups of Japanese tourists, but one lady had been asked to step back just one more step for a photo on a turret at the crusader castle, Crak des Chevaliers, and fell backwards onto a courtyard. She apparently recovered from her leg fracture, but this and other factors may have discouraged Japanese trips for a time, in fact, a long time. In Aleppo we met a Texan who worked for an oil company in Saudi Arabia. He was driving with his wife and two friends when they were detained by armed uniformed men and taken to a police station. When asked what they thought of the Arab unrest; they said they knew nothing about it and were released; this apparently was a believable answer from an American. We also met a rather brave woman American travel agent and a Hawaiian who was manager of a high-end hotel in Damascus. We believe that we and the tour agent were the last Americans to see Palmyra in its glory.

And now it is 2016 and a nightmare war becomes more complex daily. Although central Damascus itself has generally survived, Aleppo is in ruins. As we watched the news we saw our hotel, the vast covered market, the Armenian restaurant where we had dinner, all destroyed or badly damaged.

Judith Andersen
Owls Head, ME

The citadel, patiently sitting through the centuries, has been hit repeatedly. Refugees from the cities are camping in the Dead City's ruins, some in the Roman tavern. Palmyra has been savaged by Isis. The gateways have been destroyed and the Temple of Baal is flattened. Treasures have been carted out. The director of the museum was executed because he would not divulge where some treasures were hidden. And where are the children we saw skipping down the street to school holding hands? Where are the young who had dreams? Where is the candy merchant who added extra sweets to my bag with a big smile? Where was the fellow who sat patiently at the side of the road demonstrating the uses of an old fashioned grater with the style of television pitchmen hawking electronic gadgets? Where are Sharif, his wife and three daughters and where is Nour? We scan pictures of refugees nightly. There are reports that Assad dines luxuriously twice a week at the much emptier Naranj on the Street Called Straight.

***

Kate Leigh
Portsmouth, NH

Throwback

Kind of a throwback,
This morning of ice,
Slick and slushy mess.
Not enticing since
The recent breaths of
Eager nascent spring.
The way forward
Nevertheless.

Danielle Walczak
Orono, ME

July, Westport Island, Maine

At least once a day
a child spends their allowance on candy
at Fernald's.

Eyes widen and sugar is king,
the moon being queen,
I arrive when she is
full,
being only partially,
with you in a photo
tucked
behind the visor,
I am coming home.

New location
misty salt signifies
day's closing, while you
try to convince me airplanes
drop aluminum to create haze,
convince me carrots intend to intertwine
or brackish water is part you, part me.

Naked in the kitchen, you are
drumming.

I'm picking scabs off my raspberry rashes,
wanting your rhythm around me,
between my fingers and lips
your music is made with sticks
that are the woods I sleep in
and I wake to the fog between
coyote howls and blue moons.

Danielle Walczak
Orono, ME

In the morning, turkeys are falling from trees
ripping weeds
paintbrushes on wood trunks
piano from a sleepy town hall
gas stove igniting
gear change at the hills
or swells

I'm putting your pieces together by sound.
Keep playing.

***

Mark D. Biehl
Hales Corners, WI

The Candidate/Ship of State

She entered the room under full sail,
Tacking with purpose and agility.
Her findings and trim a diamond glint
With a hint of spinnaker crimson
Reaching over her bow.

The guests parted
To allow her space, and in her gentle wake
Rushed forward to make contact.

Gradually the tide of attraction
Receded, and
Weighing anchor with a final promise,
She caught the swelling waves of well-wishers
And slipped away with fading recognition.

Zibette Dean
Edgecomb, ME

George's Boat

My mother, waking in
her assisted-living place,
asked, *Where is this hotel?*
her own rooms having
become unfamiliar
while she slept.

I said, *It's your own apartment.*
She looked round at the one
wall of windows, neutral paint,
the one framed photograph.
Oh yes, she said, *there's George's boat.*

The boat Dad grew up with,
kept around in photographs and stories.
Part of my father lived always
in the cockpit of that boat.

***

Patrick T. Randolph
Lincoln, NE

High School Story of Bell, Book, and Candle

Who really cared if
She was a witch inside an
English teacher's clothes?

She turned my "F"s into "A"s
With that sultry silent glance!

Robert Cawley
Las Vegas, NV

The Last Picture Show

On the morning of January 27, 1951 a gigantic atomic blast was set off at a test range located at Yucca Flats in Nevada. The giant pink cloud that rose from that blast slowly made its way east until it returned to earth in the form of deadly fallout. No one seemed to be alarmed what the radiation from this fallout would do to people living in the areas of St. George and nearby Snow Canyon, Utah.

The horror that was to follow was not revealed until the years of 1984 and 1991.

In 1954 the fabled Howard Hughes ended his career as a producer with this movie titled, *The Conqueror* starring John Wayne, Susan Hayward, Pedro Armendariz and Agnes Moorhead. The film was directed by multi-talented Dick Powell. The film was based on vague information on the life of Mongol leader Genghis Kahn (played by John Wayne). This high-budget oriental western started shooting on locations in Snow Canyon and around St. George, Utah in August 1954.

The cast and crew numbered two hundred and twenty plus many native Americans from a nearby Indian reservation who acted as Mongol horsemen. Everyone knew about the radiation but no one thought it was serious. For thirteen weeks they were exposed to the radiation in days of 120 degree heat and nights and mornings of bitter cold as the film sought to duplicate the Gobi Desert. When they completed location filming and returned to the studio for re-takes and supplemental shots they took sixty tons of the radiated dust and dirt with them to be placed on the sound stages where they worked.

Four years after the picture was completed Pedro Armendariz was diagnosed with kidney cancer and killed himself when he was told his condition was terminal.

From 1954 until 1984, ninety-one of the cast and crew of

Robert Cawley
Las Vegas, NV

two-hundred twenty developed various types of cancer and over half of them including Wayne, Hayward and Morehead had died. Michael and Patrick Wayne, sons of star John Wayne, had accompanied their father to the location. Michael developed skin cancer and later died and his brother Patrick had a breast tumor removed.

St. George residents have been exposed for years to the radiation in the ground and water and the residents have contracted cancer in huge numbers.

Howard Hughes, who only visited the set for brief intervals, was said to be shocked and disturbed about what had happened in Utah. He withdrew the film from distribution until 2006 when it was released as a DVD.

Hughes never produced another film so for him and for many of his cast and crew it was truly the "last picture show."

***

A. McKinne Stires
Westport Island, ME

The Victim

The day began like freshly baked bread,
full and steamy, puffed with promise and pleasure.
As the sun cruised from its brilliant debut
through increasing clouds, and the bread cooled,
several hungers were appeased, but not mine.

The last crumb fell away, late in a stormy night,
and was scuffed to the trash in the subway tracks
where a stuffed, humped-backed rat
snatched the crumb with a lightning tongue
and snuffled my last morsel of hope.

Donna Bruno
Ft. Lauderdale, FL

Whose Hands Are These?

Whose hands are these?
     wrinkled, arthritic, and blue-veined
Trembling—spilling everything they hold
       fingers stiff and gnarled
     Useless for buttoning
How long have they been thus?
     Which once were smooth and creamy
       fragrant with lavender-scented lotion
"Oh! so very soft!" he used to say
     But strong enough
       To hoist a precious babe upon the hip
     And lift the weighty pot
       From off the blackened grate
To scrub on corrugated wash boards
     Come laundry day
And vigorously sweep
       The floorboards inside and the porch outside
Grab oozing udders in the barn
     To milk the bursting, swollen-bellied cows
Then lug laboriously
     Splashing, weighty pails across the frozen
     ground
These hands were never idle
     Knitting, mending, sewing—come eventide
       Cooking, cleaning, child-ing by day
Do they remember?
     That soon will be forever still.

Janet N. Gold
Camden, ME

Scars on the Bark

Dying and being born
is how I've spent my time
on all the trails among
the startled footprints
of the deer I know
have passed this way before me.

Dying a little here
sometimes there
and then turning
to gaze following a sound
a breath from the forest
where birches unfurl verses
and roots endlessly tangle
passing their stories around.

Dying because that's how we live
each small death a lesson learned
then forgotten
because the buck has rubbed his antlers on the oak
and I saw the scars on the bark
and I knew the wonder
like no other
that leaves you free of words
leaves you coming into being.

Discover. Creation.
We think we are making
when it is finding
we're about. It's all there,
isn't it? Has been all along.

(continued)

Janet N. Gold
Camden, ME

But such beauty
cannot be held for long. And so
I die a little here
sometimes there
so I may again be born.

***

Joan Peck Arnold
South Berwick, ME

The Filly

Before she was a teen-ager
she was a horse.
One day Arabian, the next
dappled gray or Lipizzaner.

Slapping her thigh,
she galloped over meadows,
jumped barriers and boulders,
splashed through a stony stream
to grass greening in the sun.

Decked out in riding silks of pastel plaid,
she raced the track at Hialeah
where stately day-glo pink
flamingos stomped and strutted
like Philadelphia mummers on New Year's Day.

She turned into the wind, and headed for home,
then tethered the reins to a paddock fence,
and cantered in the kitchen door,
nickering.

Margaret Yocom
Farmington, ME

Rafting Up

In memory of my father,
Norman Davidheiser Yocom (1923–2016)

Four loons float east down the lake
A fifth surfaces
Then another, and another.
One sweeps its neck left, and right

One dips its beak, and dives
One looks back—the rowan, its red berries
One hoots to an unseen eighth
Then another, and another.

We hover around him
One perches on the windowsill, one on the bed
One sways side to side in the chair
One stands on one leg, then the other.

Soon we will dust off our black shoes
Our black dresses, our suits
We will fasten white pearls around our necks
We will stiffen white collars

We will walk down the aisle to the front pew
We will track each other, glance by glance
We will sing one song
Then another, and another.

Jon D. Olsen
Jefferson, ME

Celebrating Baseball

"Dad, can I get another ball?" Jonny asked showing him the one in tatters from too many impacts on gravel.

"Sure, go ahead son," he replied, and Jonny went up to the ell above the kitchen where all kinds of stuff lay in boxes from our 1949 move from California to Melrose, Massachusetts, and then up to Jefferson, Maine. Dad had just retired from the Navy after 20 years, including World War II from start to finish. He and my mother had just purchased the farm on East Pond Road that had been the home to two elderly brothers born around the Civil War era. The house, barn, and related other buildings preceded even that time.

There was a single light bulb in the house and one in the barn, a party phone line in which every call had to be made through an operator, and an unlit, unheated outhouse at the end of the woodshed.

I hated it, as did my poor mother, who, like me, was used to normal indoor plumbing. It was cold, dark, and stinky, and I recall questioning my parents' wisdom for purchasing this place. But it came with around 90 acres of land, including four fields, woodlands, and shore property. Once we got a well and modern plumbing, I accepted it as home.

About a month or two after the move, at 7 1/2, I got a baby brother, Gary, but he couldn't play with me, so I was still lonesome.

Dad had joined the Navy when he was 17, in 1929, just before the stock market crash of Oct. 29, 1929, exactly twenty years to the day before Gary made his first appearance on the world stage. By the end of July, 1952, I had two more brothers, Jeff and Rick.

While in the Navy, Dad had gotten to travel the world—North Africa, the Caribbean, and Philippines, to name a few. He was in demand as a southpaw pitcher for the improvised

Jon D. Olsen
Jefferson, ME

Navy teams that would challenge any of the local talent they could find. Those are likely the happiest years for Dad—pre December 1941—of his long life. It was customary to give the winning game ball to the pitcher as a souvenir, and Dad had a box full of them, maybe thirty or forty. One by one my brothers and I got to use them until none were left.

Among our happiest times were when we kinds would ask Dad to "tap a few" in the front yard. It was there that Dad would receive our lobbed pitches with bat in hand, rarely missing, and we honed our skills in throwing accurately and agilely fielding his grounders, pop-ups, and line drives—all from short punch swings in an area not more than eighty feet. It was there too that Dad and I would play catch and he taught me to pitch. Occasionally he would throw me a "wicked" knuckleball that I could never master. This mystery pitch is unpredictable to batter, catcher, and even the pitcher once released.

It was during this time that I was, with great elation, introduced to actual organized baseball for young boys—Little League, after which was what was called PONY League (an acronym for Protect Our Nation's Youth), later renamed Babe Ruth League. These experiences constituted our "field of dreams," as they far exceeded in both form and content the numerous pick-up games in town fields with six or eight boys or the always short school recess games. Like my dad, I pitched, but also got to play every one of the nine positions during my three year Little League career. As a result of Dad's expert training in this quintessential American sport, I was deemed good enough to make the All-Star team each of these years, with the last being on the team that Dad himself coached, the Wildcats. Subsequently all three brothers followed the same trajectory, and playing in the All-Star games as well. Gary had the good fortune to be in a Maine State championship Babe Ruth team from this area. Then we all played for Lincoln Academy. Jeff played again as a pitcher, some college ball at U Maine, Orono, and both he and Gary

Jon D. Olsen
Jefferson, ME

played what is referred to as "semi-pro" ball for the pure joy and camaraderie of it all.

Each 4th of July, at the Jefferson Village School playground, there was an annual baseball game when the married men challenged the unmarried men, and a good portion of the town would turn out to cheer on the grassy bank above the field. Dad played in the early years, but time took its toll and then we brothers played. My last time was in 1970 when I was back for the summer from Hawai'i with my then new bride. I pitched for the married men and Jeff for the unmarried. While at bat, I called out to Jeff, "Put it right there," indicating belt high over the plate. He obliged and I hit it over the far driveway for a home run. The next inning he duplicated the feat against my pitch.

As Dad's playing days receded into memory, he took solace in his beloved Red Sox who had not won a World Series since the year Ted Williams was born, 1918, when Dad was seven. He endured the "almosts" in 1967 with Yastremski at his peak and the abysmal failure of 1986 with the infamous slow roller through the legs of first baseman Bill Buckner. But he hung around long enough to see the eventual triumphs in 2004 when three generations of Olsens, including my teenage son, was present with us, and in 2007.

He made it to mid-November 2008, just three weeks short of his 97th birthday in December. His mind was lucid as ever, still with humor, but with body failing. In the end it was his choice to go out on his own terms, refusing food and water and fading out in bed at home with hospice care in the final days. We miss him.

In the summer of 2015, I got a phone call. The man's voice said, "Are you the same Jon Olsen who played in the Waldoboro Little League in 1952?" I said, "Indeed I am."

"Well," he said, "the Little League state championships are being held this year in Waldoboro and we want to honor the pioneers, the charter members of the Waldoboro Little League. Will you come?"

Jon D. Olsen
Jefferson, ME

I readily assured him that I would be delighted to do so. On the assigned day, I arrived with brothers Gary and Jeff, and we, the pioneers of '52 were all given fine commemorative baseball caps announcing our status as charter members and introduced onto the field one by one—some twenty of us still extant and able to come. Most of these guys I had not seen since Little League days. Afterward, I was asked if I would come the following day to throw out the ceremonial first pitch, and I told him it was an honor and I would gladly do so.

Upon arrival I warmed up a bit, then took the mound to applause, tipping my precious hat as if I were a prized relief pitcher instead of an aging has-been. I took a pitcher's stance, stared in at my Little League catcher, the same position I held sixty one years before. I wound up like a real pitcher, and 73 year old Jonny threw a strike at the knees.

***

Eileen Hugo
Spruce Head, ME & Stoneham, MA

Sea Smoke

Sea smoke bubbles in the cove
rises just beyond the trees
a misty curtain screening
me from sea.
When from a clearing sky
sun fractures the screen into
light, radiates bars of
of fog, and finally
brings down the curtain
with a brilliant burst.

Maude Olsen
South Bristol, ME

The Awakening

A gentle breeze bestirs the trees,
        Soft pines just out my window;
For a brief moment all is still;
Not even a rustle down the hill
        to flutter the spread of oak above
        nor stir the static stream below.

Hark! A distant hammer sounds
        Beyond the sprinkle of rooftops
        and the fading yellows of Spring.
A chickadee lands in the gutter
For a drink of water, or to announce
        the feeder is empty!
A truck passes by on the road below,
        A blaring ambulance follows,
While on high a soaring osprey measures
        the sky as, far below, a boat drifts by.
Another day is on its way!!!

***

P. C. Moorehead
North Lake, WI

Wood and Sun

The sun,
moving dankly across the day,
lurches drunk
against the dark water of the wood.
A light shines on the surface—a gleam.
The wood and sun are one.

Goose River Anthology, 2016//131

Celine Rose Mariotti
Shelton, CT

The Soldier of the Vietnam War

The soldier of the Vietnam War,
He was treated so brutally,
People spat on him when he returned home,
So much pain and suffering keep him alone,
A victim of society,
He is a hero,
He fought for his country,
He was on the battlefield,
On the front lines,
People denied him the commendations he so richly deserved,
Among people he was reserved,
He didn't talk about 'Nam,
He knew how ostracized he would be,
No one cared about his duty,
His fight for other people's liberty,
He kept it in his heart,
The visions of war,
A war of a divided people,
So like Korea was in 1950,
No one would care,
To talk of his service, he had fear,
He kept it in his heart,
The buddies he lost,
The sight of blood,
The cries of anguish,

He visits that Vietnam Memorial,
And leaves a rose or a letter,
And says a prayer for those who never came home.

Frances Henkel
Wauwatosa, WI

Perfect Imperfection

Like
the grain
of sand
that causes
the oyster
to form the
lustrous pearl,
life's little
irritants,
enameled
with mercy,
fashion
the
iridescent
gem
of
charity.

***

P. C. Moorehead
North Lake, WI

Friend

If I could save a part of you,
it would be
this day, this time, this hour.

If I could leave the world to you,
it would be
this place, this space, this time.

Robert B. Moreland
Pleasant Prairie, WI

Fourth of July

They hung yellow ribbons with hope
tried to be brave, their only son.
The news there is bleak, mother cries;
son goes, a battle to be won.

Heartland summer, asphalt simmers
ship of state, who is in command?
Economy flounders, we watch
helpless while greed sets the demand.

Hope began to tarnish with fear,
her husband laid off, lost his job.
Hard workers always, he swept floors
while retirement accounts were robbed.

June twentieth, the phone call came
her knees went weak, he held her near.
Flag draped casket, life changes now.
Did it matter? Inter one dear.

Heartland summer, asphalt simmers
while retirement accounts were robbed.
Flag draped casket, life changes now;
tried to be brave, their only son.

Diane Kane
Phillipston, MA & York, ME

The God of Honey: A Love Story

At eighty-nine Stuart didn't think much about the difficulties of caring for his wife Honey. Last year the doctors told him Honey had dementia. They didn't need to tell him. He knew Honey as well as he knew the palm of his own hand. He had been noticing little inaccuracies for years.

Stuart and Honey had met seventy years ago, married, built a home and raised a family. That's what people did in the 1940s. Stuart would say he and Honey had more than a marriage. They had something that a lot of people simply never find. They had true love.

Stuart didn't just build a home seventy years ago. He built a homestead. All he needed to do was look out his front window to behold the fruits of his labors. Over to the right past his two story red barn sat his son's house. A sturdy log cabin constructed from the oaks grown and felled on his own property some forty years ago. Past the field of summer hay, lay the winding dirt road that led to his grandson's house. In the fall he could see the smoke billowing up from the chimney. When the leaves fell from the trees he could see the lights of the house in the chill of the night. His grandson had a fine wedding about ten years back, right in the yard where Stuart had got down on his knee and asked Honey to marry him in another lifetime.

Life hadn't always been easy. Sometimes he had wondered if it ever was. Honey had lost two children in the early years. They lay in the family cemetery on the edge of the hayfield. Many a tear had washed those little stones—side by side, heart by heart. The next pregnancy had nearly taken Honey.

The doctor said it was in God's hands. God was kind that day. He spared Honey and gave Stuart a son to carry his name. Those were hard times but they never went hungry.

Diane Kane
Phillipston, MA & York, ME

They farmed the land and raised cows and pigs. Chickens for eggs and horses to lighten the work load all earned their keep. His son grew strong and prospered on the farm. Honey was the mesh that held them all together with a smile and a prayer.

Stuart often wondered what would have become of him without Honey. He'd never admit it but many times his faith in God had waivered. He wondered if there was a God, why good people have to suffer.

"It's not for us to question, Stuart," she would say. "Only to believe and we will be rewarded."

Sometime Stuart wondered if the reward was worth the suffering. He would never say that to Honey. When he looked into her eyes, he knew he would suffer anything for her and never question the price. If Honey believed in God that was enough for him. He only hoped God would watch over his Honey.

Whenever the trials of life weighed heavy on Stuart's shoulders he only needed to look to Honey for reassurance. No matter what happened, Honey's response was always, "Well, it could be worse!"

When Stuart heard the strength of belief in her voice it was hard to disagree.

Stuart stayed with Honey all the time now. He never left her. It was true there was plenty of family nearby that would come over anytime. Stuart knew it would confuse Honey and he didn't want to frighten her.

When Stuart went to the store, he brought Honey with him. He used to bring her in the store. Lately, the people and noise were too much for her to handle, so he left her in the car where she was perfectly content.

Honey had always been a knitter. She knitted afghans for her son and his wife for Christmas and special occasions. She knitted baby blankets for the two grandchildren when they were born. She even knitted for the neighbors grandchildren. He couldn't remember the last time she knitted any-

Diane Kane
Phillipston, MA & York, ME

thing. Yet the knitting needles still lay beside her chair in the living room with a skein of yarn connected to them. Sometimes she would pick them up and set them in her lap. They seemed to give her comfort. Stuart started bringing them in the car with them. He would set them in her lap and say, "Honey, why don't you work on this beautiful afghan while I go in the store." She would smile and pick them up. When he returned sometime later with the groceries, not a stitch was taken. Honey would still be smiling. Stuart would tell her what wonderful work she was doing.

One day it had taken a particularly long time in the grocery store. The checkout line had been long and slow. Stuart politely thanked the young clerk and hurried to the door. He didn't notice the wrinkle in the mat by the exit. He tripped and came crashing down on the floor. He jumped up gingerly and started to gather his scattered groceries. His leg came out from under him again. It seemed as though everyone in the store had heard the ruckus and was at his side. The manager came out of his office and insisted that Stuart allow him to call the ambulance so he could be checked out. Stuart thanked him kindly. He insisted he was fine, just a bump, no need for a fuss. All the workers and customers had picked-up and re-bagged Stuart's groceries. They carried his groceries and helped him out to his car. He breathed a sigh of relief when he saw Honey sitting comfortably in her seat smiling at the knitting needles in her lap. He reassured all the kind people that he was just fine. The manager made him promise to call if he needed anything at all.

When Stuart got home he gently got Honey out of the car and into her chair in the parlor. He was hobbling back to retrieve his groceries, when his son Stu happened to look out his kitchen window. Stu was an EMT and even from that distance he knew something was very wrong. He hurried over as his dad lifted the last bag of groceries out of the trunk.

"What happened, Dad?"

"Oh, this limp you mean? I had a little tumble at the gro-

Diane Kane
Phillipston, MA & York, ME

cery store that's all. No need for worry."

Stu was very worried. He convinced his reluctant father that he needed to go to the hospital.

Stuart had broken his hip and would need surgery.

Stu, his wife Joyce, their son Kyle and his wife Charissa all took turns staying with Honey. The day after Stuart's surgery Charissa came to pick up Honey and take her to the hospital for a visit. They talked all the way to the hospital about the fall, the hip surgery and the recovery. Charissa was pleased with how well her gran was taking it all. Honey smiled and nodded her head.

When they pulled into the parking lot of the hospital Honey looked around.

"What are we doing here?" she demanded.

"Granny we're here to visit Granddad."

"What the heck is he doing here?"

Charissa proceeded patiently to tell Honey the whole story again as she got her out of the car and into the hospital, knowing full well that this wouldn't be the last telling of it.

They had a great visit with Stuart. He was in good spirits and so happy to see his Honey. When Charissa saw that her Gran was fading out and her Granddad looked tired, despite his attempts to hide it, she decided it was time to go.

As Charissa was helping her into her coat, Honey exclaimed, "Well it could be worse, Stuart! You could have broken your hip!"

"But Gran he did—."

"You're right, Honey," Stuart interrupted Charissa. "It can always be worse."

Honey smiled and kissed Stuart on the forehead.

When Stuart came home from the hospital he noticed that Honey had regressed. He tried to ignore the signs. He knew the time was coming when she would need to have medical care that he couldn't give her. He found a good place close by where he could see her often.

Diane Kane
Phillipston, MA & York, ME

Honey gradually disappeared into another world. Stuart continued to visit her every day. She rarely spoke. When she did it was in vague and broken sentences. Still she never seemed sad, and Stuart sat proudly by her side. He saved his tears for the ride home.

Honey was steadily fading and the doctors had been trying to prepare Stuart for the inevitable loss. He was looking into Honey's blank eyes, wondering how it could be any worse, when he heard the voice of Honey in his head say, *It could be worse, Stuart. I could have never known you and I can't imagine anything worse than that.*

"You're right Honey, it could be worse." Stuart said to the silent stranger in his wife's body.

He saw Honey's eyes dilate and a smile come to her sagging face.

"Stuart," she said. "It's so good to see you. I've missed you."

"I've missed you as well Honey," Stuart answered with surprise.

He saw her eyes slowly dilating back to her inner world.

"I love you," he said quickly.

Honey's lips moved in silence. He didn't need to hear, he knew what she had said.

A tear rolled down his cheek. He looked deeply into Honey's blank eyes. He was sure he saw something there. He knew it was the eternal light of true love.

He smiled through his tears and thanked the God of Honey.

Byron Hoot
Wexford, PA

Here Now Hold Not

Here now hold not that which cannot
be held but chooses only
to stay constantly changing
like Poseidon in his sea of change
each ebb and flow never the same
always something new left
on the shore, always something
taken back out into the depths
of the sea before it returns.
So, too, the ground I walk
does that ebb and flow which
comes over me.
                There is a touch
of eternity exquisite
that feels as if forever is real
until the grasp of time tightens
and it flees and the knotted muscles
of a forearm testament to what
no longer is but had been remains.
To hold too tightly is to hold
nothing—a touch more than
suffices to know how one is kept
by that grace that leaves nothing
untouched, unblessed. . .
Water running through a hand
is exactly the power all
have to hold what is given
constantly flowing whether
on a shore or dry land
the ebb and flow no grip
is strong enough to grasp.

Jeanne Severin-Hansen
Knightdale, NC

Star Gazer

We are all in the gutter, but some of us are looking at stars.
                                        –Oscar Wilde

Stars on a winter's night
Sing to the twice turned 25.
I lay cradled in street whose pavement
Cringes and crunches at the hour 5.
My back is pressed into a storm drain whose
Gurgles tell of tempests past. I gaze, teary eyed
As winter winds toss February garbed
branches into a season of clarity,
And the night sky stars sing to the
Twice turned 25.

***

Irene Zimmerman
Greenfield, WI

Camping Night

Waking after midnight, I venture out
to listen to the summer woods. A breeze
is bedding down in branches of white pine.

A fledgling peeps above me, subsides to feathery
silence. Beyond the clearing, trees converse
in creaks, whispers, sighs.

Not ready yet for sleep, I slipper down
the path for one last look at Silver Lake.
Her moonlit eye bewitches me till morning.

Lilli Lee Buck
Bristol, VA

The Christmas Card: December 22, 2002

"I want to send a Christmas card to Heaven,
To the one I love the best.
I couldn't help but write it out,
When I was writing all the rest.

"I want to send a letter to Heaven,
To the one who loved me most,
Because I know that's where my father is,
Among the heavenly host."

"Dear God, by some strange miracle,
Won't you send my dad this card?
Because I don't know where Heaven is,
And I don't know how far."

"Mr. Postman, I've got a special letter here,
And it needs an airmail stamp,
Because I am sending a letter to Heaven.
I have written it out by hand."

"Little girl, I can't take a letter to Heaven,
To pretend would be a sin.
Tie your card to the end of a big balloon,
And set it loose in the wild north wind."

She took the card for her father,
And tied it to a red balloon,
Then set it loose in the wild north wind,
Which whistled a mournful tune.

Lilli Lee Buck
Bristol, VA

With gusts and blasts the cold wind blew,
And carried the balloon up high,
Until it finally disappeared,
In the bleak and wintry sky.

Hundreds and hundreds of miles away,
An old man sat alone,
A sick and lonely widower,
In a cold and wretched home.

It seemed the whole world passed him by;
His children were scattered far.
No one remembered him at Christmas time,
To send him a gift or card.

He sat alone on Christmas Eve,
And wished on the Christmas Star,
That by some miracle he might receive
At least one Christmas card.

As he walked back from his empty mailbox,
What did he see on the snow?
There lay a big, bright, red balloon,
Tied up with a Christmas bow.

And dangling from it, tied with string,
He saw a Christmas card.
And there it lay upon the snow,
In the starlight in his yard.

"A Christmas card from Heaven," he said,
"Has come to me this night!
It has come to me on the wings of the wind,
To make my sad heart light."

Lilli Lee Buck
Bristol, VA

He took it into his cabin,
And opened the pretty card.
And, drawn on it, in a childish hand,
Was a big white Christmas Star.

"Dear Daddy," said the little card,
"We miss you every day.
Life has never been the same for us,
Since the night you went away.

"Dear Daddy, we still love you,
And that's all I have to say.
And I pray to God you'll get this card,
Somehow, by Christmas Day."

He looked down at the signature,
And it said, "With love from Nell."
"Why, that's my little daughter's name,
The one I love so well."

The old man in his rambling mind
Believed it was the same.
With tear-filled eyes he knelt to pray,
"All praise to Jesus' name!

"Thanks be to God for bringing me
A letter from my child,
A Christmas card that was brought to me
By the north wind cold and wild."

Amen

Flora Jackson Sawyer
Warren, ME

The Winter Thaw

Stella arrived in the summer of '48 with her precious few belongings. Sam met her at the back door, the only usable one in the old house. He took her suitcase from her with a curt greeting: "Careful of that step."

She followed him in, bent and tired, and carrying a beat-up satchel and an easel, her short brown hair mostly hidden by a large red bandana.

"Do you need help?" Bessie, Sam's wife, asked half-heartedly, knowing her sister wouldn't allow anyone to touch her art supplies.

"No thanks, I'm not an invalid yet," she replied in her raspy smoker's voice.

Oh boy, Bessie thought, *I can see she's still her independent old self. And, I can see there's still no love lost between her and Sam—Sam's stern temperament had always clashed with Stella's temperamental, artistic ways—but, anyway, he's consented to try to help her out this time, after her third divorce, and I'm glad she's here—just hope we can all survive this visit without a knock-down drag-out!* More like their mother, Lottie, who was slightly taller of stature, and more even-tempered, Bessie followed them into the house donned in a fresh house dress and tidy apron.

All six children lined up warily. Blonde, blue-eyed Norma, the oldest, and just turning twelve, stood tense, showing no emotion. Next, Lucille, examining Stella with cool brown eyes. Flora, the hazel-eyed, quiet half of the twins, stood shyly next to brown-eyed Lenora—the bolder half—who was giggling nervously. Jean, the youngest girl, now seven years old, stood waiting, curious...while little Billy, barely three, stared self-consciously at the floor.

Stella scanned the lot of them, then addressed Billy, who was clinging to his mother's knee.

Flora Jackson Sawyer
Warren, ME

"Poor little Billy, with all those big sisters. You can help me build my rabbit pens—how's that?"

Ah—the rabbit pens! Sam, willing to let her raise Angora rabbits if it meant she could pay for her board, had agreed to let Stella rebuild his old chicken coops. This was all fine until winter set in. That's when the trouble began.

"My, it's cold out there! I don't know why I can't get a little help," Stella muttered as she hauled off her snow-packed mittens and threw them on the back of the hot wood stove. Bessie grabbed them, dripping and sizzling, and draped them over the back of the warming shelf.

"Look, you didn't have to come here. You know what Maine winters are like. You should have thought of that when you decided to raise rabbits," yelled Sam from the living room.

"I'm just trying to earn my keep," she said loudly, then muttered under her breath, "I sure don't expect to get any help from you, let alone sympathy."

"I heard that! I've been working in the woods all day and who helps me?" You couldn't wait 'till I could get to it tomorrow. So if you're bound to do it yourself—go ahead." Sam's voice was rising.

Bessie looked tiredly at her sister. Stella's knit winter hat and straying strands of dark brown hair were encrusted with snow. Her thick glasses steamed up as she struggled to remove her jacket. A puddle of water encircled her heavy boots on the worn kitchen floor. *Poor Stella,* she thought, *could make plenty of money selling her paintings, but she chooses to raise Angora rabbits. Why does she insist on making herself suffer so? She ladled some corn chowder into a bowl and set it on the table.*

"This will warm you up quick. I'll cut some Johnny Cake. We've all eaten."

"No thank you, I'll just have some black coffee," she said, as she lit up a Camel, "I'm going up to bed." She coughed hoarsely. "I don't need to stay around here and listen to dis-

Flora Jackson Sawyer
Warren, ME

paraging remarks." Her large brown eyes were close to tears. "Could you bring up the coffee when it's ready?" She stumbled up the narrow back stairs and down the long, unpainted hallway to her room.

Stella came down with a cold the next day, which soon turned into pneumonia. The kids all took turns carrying her meals upstairs. Normally taking things in stride, Bessie guiltily enjoyed the temporary relief from tension, even though she knew Stella was making the most of all the attention. Prayer was an important part of Bessie's life and she depended on it now. If only she could get Stella to pray. But she had about as much hope in that area as she did for her husband, Sam. After several weeks, her sister was able to be up and about. The whole countryside was in the midst of a January thaw.

One day a gentle knock sounded at the door. Bessie handed her apron to Stella and opened the door. She escorted Rev. Ward into the living room where her husband was stoking the end heater. Stella set her kettle of water on the wood stove, and began to add a cup of raw rice. "You go ahead and visit, Bess," she said, glad for an excuse to stay in the kitchen. "I'll just finish this dessert for the kids."

But Sam was not so lucky.

"Uh, sorry, got soot on my hand," he grunted, as Rev. Ward extended his hand.

"No problem, just came by to invite you folks to the special meeting at the schoolhouse tonight."

"Well...that one-room school is pretty small. I'll just stay home—make room for someone else, Sam said as he brushed past Rev. Ward and exited the room, slamming the door behind him.

"My!" That was a little indecent of Sam," said Stella. But her rough voice melted a little as she saw her sister's face fall.

"Tell you what, Bess, if Sam goes, I'll go—how's that." She offered as the reverend left. "He certainly would never let

Flora Jackson Sawyer
Warren, ME

me out-do him, even when it comes to religion. "But don't think it'll do either of us any good, because I'm sure it won't! Now I'd better get out there and get to work on them rabbit pens while the weather's thawing, or them rats'll have my rabbits." She grabbed her flannel shirt, quickly knotted a red bandana around her unruly brown hair, and rushed out the door before she could make any more rash commitments.

Bessie smiled, picked up the apron Stella had thrown across a chair, and tied it around her waist. Glancing heavenward, she said aloud, "Guess it isn't just the weather that's thawing around here."

Then she drew a kettle of water from the old iron pump by the cast iron sink, set it on the stove and contentedly began peeling potatoes.

***

Eileen Hugo
Spruce Head, ME & Stoneham, MA

Unfettered

Black water swirls over barnacles
embossed on the tree-like legs of the wharf.
Wide weathered planks slick with moss,
hold nets, fish bins, coils of rope,
lobster traps, anchors and brass cleat leashes.
Hear the clang of the halyards
like friendly dogs, sail boats tethered to buoys
slowly squirm, waiting to be taken out for a run
waiting to be alive in the wind.
Out there on the icy sea your hair flutters
with the wind, your tanned face exultant.
You are bird and fish and foolish
in waves of wind and sea.

Paul G. Charbonneau
Rockport, ME

The Fall

May I come in,
sit with you
and share a mug or two
of freshly pressed cider,
made from deep inside
my little orchard?

Grown heavy and ripe, Cortlands,
Macs and Golden Delicious
lost their grip
and by the cartload
fell into earth's lap, asking
to be saved and squeezed

so we could sip
spring's flowering fruit,
crushed and ground,
juice to slake our thirsts,
unfiltered earthy extract
oozing from a distant core.

May I come in,
sit with you
and share a moment or two,
brought here by a force
from deep inside
my little orchard?

F. Anthony D'Alessandro
Celebration, FL

My Little Benji

I sit here in my self inflicted, invisible mentally made tunnel
wearing a hangdog look while staring at my snoozing wall
      clock
as it struggles to click and tick in agonizing slow motion.
I wonder and worry, and say to myself,
Benji, what are your thoughts?
Still seven months away from standing, nine months from
      those measured
first steps, and at this grinding, everlasting moment masked
      men and women,
clutching knives invade your baby body, barely freed from
      your umbilical cord.
You feel it, the scratch, and the sharp edges.
You are too alert. You are too bright not to notice.
What you're feeling continues to haunt my mind.
Surprise, pain, confusion, healing?
Oh how I wish I could be in gold rush country with you,
cuddling your quivering, confused hand thru this surgery.
I wish I could wave some magical wand and force the hour
hand to race 'round.
Tears cascade, soaking my workshirt in salty stain,
as I think of you in this moment.
Coraggio brave little guy.
Hopefully, our Creator will allow those blurry people in blue
to make the repairs needed, and leave it to you to heal.
Ah! Hours later you appear on my hand-held screen,
      smiling thru the pain.

Barbara Winslow
Norridgewock, ME

You Bloomed for Me

When my mind lay frozen beneath
Snows of doubt,
And my heart lay dormant
In fields of fear

When winter covered my soul
And the land was dark,
You listened
You heard me
You reached through
The ice
You gave me spring.

You rescued me from despair
You held me up
You filled me
With hope.

***

Thomas Peter Bennett
Silver Spring, MD

After Chilling Night Winds

An Evergreen! She exclaimed,
While gazing out the window,
Beyond the naked sunbathing
Maples, poplars, and oaks,
To a green, cone-shaped figure,
Waving a welcome to winter.

Barbara Ryland
South Portland, ME

French Horn Years

My adolescence
circled around love
for the French horn,
whose beautiful tubing,
curled and spiraled,
transformed my breath,
and grew wider
with each turn
until it opened,
a giant conch,
offering music
to the waiting air.

Over and over
I polished its brass,
crafted my art,
breathed deeper
and deeper
into its mysteries
until I, too,
shone and sparkled,
transfixed by its haunting sound.

Drawn by devotion,
practice became prayer,
giving, receiving
through this great cornucopia
of love.

Phoebe Nichols
Damariscotta, ME

From Away

"Are you pouting?" George asked, directing his question at Suzanne's back.

She stared glumly out the truck window at the passing scene, mostly bare trees and fields of dried tufts of something. Three days of steady rain hadn't improved things. She said nothing, punched the radio's "seek" button, cutting off Johnny Cash in mid-phrase, and attempted to tune in a scratchy public radio station.

"It's no good," he said. "We're halfway between Portland and Bangor. It's country or nothing around here."

"I still don't see why we had to come up here *today*. I wanted to have lunch at that quaint little lighthouse place we saw yesterday. All we've passed today are truck stops. Who does that old fart think he is, telling you what *day* you can buy antiques from him? Is he in *business*, or isn't he?"

"Oh, Wallace is in business all right. Wait till you meet him. We're almost there. See? Here's the paper mill. Most of the locals work here."

The dark bulk of the paper mill was the only manmade object in sight. It looked deserted except for three tall stacks spewing long flattened ribbons of gray smoke. As they came around a curve in the road, a lonesome traffic light signaled them to a stop, and an empty logging truck pulled out of the mill's main gate and turned north onto the state road. The driver nodded at George and lifted his index finger from the steering wheel in greeting. George responded with a similar gesture.

"What was that about?" Suzanne asked.

"Oh, that was Leon Campbell. We went to high school together. His whole family drives those big trucks, even his mother—in the summers anyway."

"Do you know *everyone* in this state?"

Phoebe Nichols
Damariscotta, ME

"Anyone who *is* anyone, I do," he grinned.

His old truck bounced sharply as it met a deep pothole, the work of a hard winter and a spring thaw.

"You okay? It's mud season here, you know. Anywhere else, it'd be Spring by now. Come on over here, why don't you?"

He reached over and ruffled her curly red hair. After a minute, she slid across the bench seat and rested her head against his shoulder, then propped her feet up on the dashboard and closed her eyes. He glanced down at her and smiled to himself. She looked as peaceful as a sleeping child, so unlike the first time he'd seen her, pacing back and forth beside her disabled sports car with her cell phone to her ear and traffic whipping by. George had pulled over, and after assuring her he was not a thug—producing his driver's license and an old library card as identification, she'd relaxed a bit and let him change the flat tire, while they chatted about this and that. After he'd stowed her tire and jack in the trunk and wiped his hands, they'd exchanged all the usual— one phone number in his case, and two in hers—plus her e-mail addresses and website. Her business card stated "Suzanne Ripley, Financial Consultant" with a Manhattan address. Although he'd been thinking about her from time to time during the following week—something about her Susan Saranden good looks was very appealing to George—he'd been surprised when she called him.

"How about going out to dinner with me—as a reward for helping a woman in distress? It'll be my treat—well I can expense it, since I was on my way to a meeting with clients that day. What do you say? Next Thursday?"

So they'd gone to a place Suzanne knew, part Mexican cantina, part gay bar, and the festive atmosphere was contagious. Or maybe it was the wine—at any rate they'd ended up taking a cab to his sublet for more coffee, and she'd spent the night. Later, they'd joke about "attorney-client privileges."

George's friend, Phil, a retired Army shrink, had once

Phoebe Nichols
Damariscotta, ME

presented him with a theory about "lovemaps" to explain why George always tended to fall for a certain type of woman. According to a sexologist named Dr. Money, humans are imprinted early in their formative years with a sort of blueprint for their ideal sex partner.

As Phil phrased it, "Remember Konrad Lorenz and the baby geese that followed him every where, thinking he was their mommy because he was the first living thing they ever saw? Well, I'm just saying that you seem to have a thing for redheads. Maybe you should change your name to Charlie Brown."

"Yeah, the Little Red-Haired Girl he always lusted after," said George. "There might be some validity to that." He thought back to his high school girl friend, Donna May Johnson—red hair, petite build, yet mentally kind of tough—and a whiz at math. She'd gotten a full scholarship to MIT, and the last he'd heard, she'd married some guy from Kansas or Nebraska and never looked back. There were other women as well. He could see how Suzanne Ripley kind of fit the mold.

They'd been spending most of their free time together ever since that first night, usually at her small, starkly modern apartment on East 88th Street and this was the first time he'd brought her back to Maine to see the old house he was renovating. His enthusiasm about the place was obvious, and they'd arranged and rearranged furniture on their first night there. A wish list had evolved, resulting in this trek inland to see the old man.

Wallace Clayborne would have some wonderful piece—he usually did—and they'd be getting it near the beginning of the cycle from an old woman's house to a picker's barn, to a country auction to a high-priced antique show, and finally to a Park Avenue living room. Wally also dealt in jewelry. He kept the stuff in cigar boxes and mayonnaise jars in his china closet and he always knew the daily price of gold. George had hinted to him on the phone the night before that

Phoebe Nichols
Damariscotta, ME

he might be in the market for a nice piece of jewelry.

They pulled into town, past a factory that produced high tech running shoes, which were mostly shipped out of state to people who took their exercise seriously, then past "Linda's Redemption Center" and down the hill. Wally's old gray house stood next to a Pentecostal church, surrounded by a low chain link fence. The deeply rutted and muddy driveway was clogged with vans and pickup trucks. An old man in a dirty parka supervised as a teenager with a sparse mustache buffed the hood of a blue Chevy van.

"Hey, Pete! How ya been?" The old man ambled over to George's side of the pickup and rested his knobby hand on the door frame.

"Sorry to hear 'bout your father, George. Terrible way to go. We'll surely miss him."

"Thanks, Pete. How's Wally doin'?"

"He's had a bout with his heart, and Erlene's after him to slow down, but he's good. Same old Wally. Go on in. He's in the parlor.

"That your girlfriend?" Pete asked in a stage whisper, craning his neck for a better look at the attractive redhead.

"She's actually my accountant, Pete. Suzanne—I want you to meet an old friend of mine."

"How d'you do ma'am? Old Georgie here used to help us out at auctions when he was just a kid. We could still use him, if he ever gets tired of the big city and decides to come on home."

"I don't see how anyone could get tired of New York—it's the center of the universe!" said Suzanne, getting out of the truck and slamming the door.

George noticed she had brought a copy of the *Wall Street Journal* with her, which she carried under her arm. She was wearing slim black slacks and a cashmere turtleneck sweater, in spite of it being April already. She hadn't really felt warm since they'd left the city.

This issue of New York vs. Maine wasn't new to them.

Phoebe Nichols
Damariscotta, ME

They'd debated it regularly since the first night they met. He lived in the city because that was where the jobs were, but he often had a hard time with the people he encountered there. They seemed so blatantly aggressive to him, the way they drove, or shopped, or lined up for movies, always looking for the little crack in the other guy's armor, ready to make their move. Suzanne was happiest when she was working, figuring out some way to beat the system on behalf of a client. He had to admit she'd saved him a bundle this year, but then, her fees were pretty steep, too. He had optimistically thought she'd fall in love with Maine on her first visit, maybe want to settle down here, maybe with him. And she'd loved what she'd seen so far, but they hadn't strayed more than ten miles from open ocean until today. The coast was for photographers, tourists, and rich people. The other Maine was George's home territory, the part that looked raw and ugly half the year, overridden with mosquitoes and black flies for most of the spring and summer, but was heaven on earth from August through October. By then, the tourists were heading back to New Jersey and Massachusetts, the nights were crisp and cool, and the sky was a deep cloudless blue all day long.

As they stepped onto the narrow glassed-in porch leading to Erlene Clayborne's kitchen, George did a double take at a spare suit of Wally's working clothes, draped on a hanger, with a faded blue cap promoting the local Chevy dealer hanging from the same nail. Looked just like the old boy himself, short and wide and well-used. Through the glass panels of the inner door he saw Erlene scrubbing her patterned linoleum and as he walked inside, the strong odor of Lysol greeted him.

"Georgie! You snuck up on me, you devil!" She propped her mop against a light green painted cupboard and threw her arms around him. Then, releasing him, she nodded at Suzanne as George introduced them.

"That driveway's a disaster! Do you have a paper towel or

Phoebe Nichols
Damariscotta, ME

something I can clean off my shoes with?" Without a word, Earlene handed her the whole roll.

Frowning, Suzanne sat in the brown vinyl recliner by the window and scraped clots of black mud off her leather flats while the older woman mopped up the footprints she'd trailed across the floor.

"Care for some coffee or tea?" Erlene asked them. Suzanne shook her head and George, remembering Erlene's coffee, chose tea. She disappeared into the pantry and he heard the hum of a microwave oven, then the bell. When she returned, she handed him a heavy mug.

"Red Zinger! Erlene, have you gone Granola on me?"

"I don't keep any caffeine in the house on account of Wally's heart. It's hard enough to get him to rest now and then. What have you been doin' with yourself?"

"Well, I'm about half finished with that consulting project I told you about before, and then I've been thinking about moving my office back here. The house is coming along pretty good, and I've got enough work to keep me out of trouble. I've been trying to talk Suzie into coming with me, but I don't know. She's having trouble sleeping up here. Says it's too quiet."

At the sound of her name, Suzanne momentarily looked up from her reading. "Quiet? I'll say it's quiet—it's like a damned morgue! The whole place shuts down after dark. And don't call me Suzie."

She hadn't recovered from her mood yet, and realizing she'd be engrossed in the paper for some time, he got up, set his mug in the sink and wandered into the front room where Wally was conducting business with several other men. George recognized a couple of them.

"Well, if it ain't the Prodigal Son! Still makin' it big in New York City?"

"Hey, Wally—how's it going?"

"Can't complain—no one listens."

A tall white-haired man with a serious black mustache

Phoebe Nichols
Damariscotta, ME

had assembled a couple of carved decoys, a mantel clock, and a stack of old books and was trying to negotiate a price for the lot. "You must think I fell off a potato truck! Can't you do better than that, Wally?"

Wally Clayborne pushed his cap back up his forehead, then spit tobacco juice into a coffee can while he considered.

"That Edgar Rice Burroughs is a first edition, Ronny. You could turn right around and make it all back on that, but I'll tell you what I'll do. Here's what I'll do. You take this other duck as well, and I'll throw in the postcard album for another one sixty-five."

The dealer groaned and rolled his eyes, but he pulled a roll of bills from his shirt pocket and peeled off several hundreds, which he handed over to the old man. Then he picked up his goods and left the house.

George noticed that the floral wallpaper was still ripped and hanging down in places. He'd once asked the old man about it and Wally had said he'd done it on purpose, in case the tax assessor ever paid him a visit. The other buyers finished hammering out deals while George poked around the parlor. Nothing was marked; the prices were all in Wally's head, so the process was slow. A folding aluminum table set up against the fireplace held a few choice pieces of Chinese porcelain, a plastic bag containing a handful of silver spoons, and an Aunt Jemima cooky jar, but today George was looking for furniture. An inlaid chest of drawers caught his eye and he looked it over closely for clues to its age and origin.

"Say, Wally, what's the story on this?" He tried to sound casual, but his blood pressure was rising. He was pretty sure the chest was eighteenth century, maybe early, and it was in fairly good condition.

"That's somethin' ain't it? Got it out of a house in Dover-Foxcroft. It's been in the same family for two hundred years!"

"It's pretty nice. Those aren't the original brasses, are they? And what about the feet? Do you think they've been replaced?"

Phoebe Nichols
Damariscotta, ME

"Hell, no! Pete and I gave it a good going over. We even put the black light to it. It's not American, but I think it's good. I was thinkin' about savin' it for my July 4th auction. Some collector from out-of-state ought to pay big money for that!"

"What do you think it'll bring—a thousand?"

"More like two or three, I'd say. That's a rare piece. If you're looking for a bureau, I've got something out in the shed you ought to see. Pete, take George out back and show him the chest that fella brought by this morning."

He wasn't that interested in looking at anything else, but it was all part of the game when it came to dealing with old timers like Wally, so he followed Pete out through the ell to the old garage. Although the house was right in town, its many connected outbuildings spoke of its farmhouse origins. As they passed through the kitchen, George stopped by Suzanne's chair.

"Come on out. Pete's got a bureau to show us."

She slipped her stained shoes back on and followed the men through a series of hallways separated by a variety of doors.

"George, how much longer is this going to take? I thought we could have some fun today—go shopping or visit some of your friends."

"Shh, Suzie! We *are* shopping and these are my friends. This won't take too much longer—and then we can go out for lunch. I know a funny little place near here."

"Funny—right. I can hardly wait."

As he'd suspected, the bureau was nothing special, just something that could have been pictured in a Sears catalog around 1900. Suzanne found it charming, however.

"George, this would be perfect in your apartment! You could paint it white and use it in the dining room."

Old Pete didn't say a word, but George suspected he wouldn't approve of slapping paint onto a lovely piece of golden oak.

Phoebe Nichols
Damariscotta, ME

"If you really love it, Suze, I'll buy it for you and you can put it in *your* apartment. Will you take seventy-five, Pete? It's a deal, then. Give me a hand and I'll load it right on the truck. Suzanne, why don't you wait for me out here? I just want to speak with Wally for a second. I'll be right out."

The other buyers had concluded their business and gone off, and Wally was alone in the small room between the kitchen and the parlor. He sat on the faded sofa that faced the TV, looking through a stack of photos. He and Pete documented all the best antiques that passed through their hands, and sometimes he liked to look through the pictures again.

"Remember this weathervane, George? I think it might have been the best thing I ever had."

"Yeah, I remember it. That Pennsylvania guy—what's his name—he bought it, didn't he? It was a beauty."

"Good to see you again, George. You moving back soon?"

"Probably this summer if I can tie up all the loose ends. Maybe I'll get up for your auction and steal that chest of drawers away from you." He got out his checkbook and began to scratch out a check. "Let me pay you for that oak dresser right now. I'd better get going."

"I've got some beautiful jewelry in the other room. Want to take a look? There's an emerald ring that would go real good with red hair." The old man winked at him.

"Nah, I'm in no hurry," said George, putting away his checkbook.

Stephen Goldfinger
West Newton, MA

Newton Cemetery: May 10, 2009

Bloomsbury somehow captures it:
Magnolia azalea dogwood lilac
Once climaxed this season for those below,
Stirred their living souls.
Now they lie deep,
Insensate to birdsong
Windsong
Watersong.

In the section of the visited.

Sprays of red, white, lavender, yellow
Flags for the veterans
Muted voices
Footprints.
Sanchez Levy Moy Shevarian
Kostopoulous Brodsky Liang Vahedi
McTiernan Ferrari
Sarkissian Bronzo Mandell Hunt
And four-in-a-row: Panaggio Chin Hassan McDonald.
Carved sharp and deep.

The domain of the ancients.

Grizzled headstones.
Noiseless
Flowerless
Flagless
Untrodden.
Enos Currier Winward Warren
Tarbox Lowell (a reverend) Higginson Crocker

(continued)

Stephen Goldfinger
West Newton, MA

Brock (Missionary to the Tulugus South India)
Almy Fairley Hawthorne
SF Smith "Author of My Country 'Tis of Thee"

A walk from present to past
And into my future.

***

Margaret Yocom
Farmington, ME

On the Path to the Sea, Kennebunkport, Late October

The entire year hangs on the wild beach roses.
All over the throat-high bushes
clumps of rosehips sway

some plump, still red and fruited
some collapsed, leaking
some dry, leather brown and dreaming of snow.

Along the lawn of the shuttered gray house,
wild roses stood guard all summer.
Their green and growing branches, flush with thorns,

flanked the gray gate,
gave truth to the red-lettered warning: PRIVATE
All those who slept inside felt the promise—

a summer that would last a hundred years,
every day, roses, blush pink,
with a fragrance like forever.

Anne Cyr
Buxton, ME

The Chestnut Tree

Every October in my hometown
our church had a harvest fair.
My mother made a vat of baked beans
that simmered overnight, filling our house
with a delectable smell.
Delivered the next morning,
they were served as part of the luncheon
on long tables with white cloths in the parish hall,
where ancient rippling windowpanes
let in the autumn light.

The soaring church foyer was filled
with buckets of fall weeds,
sold for dried arrangements.
I helped collect these weeds from empty lots:
milkweed, tall grasses, tansy,
golden rod, yarrow,
teasel, bittersweet.
Their combined scent made me giddy.

Games of chance were set up
in the stalls of the carriage house,
and tables on the lawn groaned
with baked goods and caramel apples.
We kept running back to our mothers—
arrayed in aprons in the kitchen—
and begged them for more money,
promising to do more chores.

Anne Cyr
Buxton, ME

As the day wore on, I made my way
to the front of the church,
where a solitary horse-chestnut tree glowed
as if clothed in a yellow gown,
its ripening fruit encased in burr-like husks,
falling to the ground. I would scavenge
the large round smooth mahogany nuts,
stow them in my pocket, add them
to my treasures at home.

A quarter century later
I return to the old church
for my mother's memorial service.
Held in the stark sanctuary, white-paned windows
let in the clear September light.
One after another, people stand
in their pews to pay tribute. They speak
of her wit, her wisdom, her contributions
to society, to the church.

Later, after the reception,
I seek out the chestnut tree,
discover a bounty of nuts in the grass below.
The whitish patch on their shells
are shaped like hearts.
I fill my pockets.

Back home, I put them in a jug
and tuck it high on a shelf
among vases, blue bottles, duck decoys.
Come spring, I drag out a stepladder
and take the jug down to dust it,
then shake it gently to hear the chestnuts
clank against the ceramic sides—
shake it just hard enough
to bring her back.

Helen Ackermann
Rothschild, WI

Someone Else to Love You

Walking between her parents,
the bride approached the altar.
A kiss by the father and one by
the mother, the groom then
ready to take her to the altar.

Vows are exchanged,
rings are slipped on fingers,
a blessing given and soon the
announcement. "I present to you
Mr. and Mrs. Gerald Brown. Jerry,
you may kiss the bride."

Those gathered, clap their hands
as the couple begins the journey down
the aisle and out into the bright sunlight.

Years ago, I remember thinking, at your
wedding, "I am pleased that you have someone who
loves you as much as I do." But that
was years ago.

Now you tell me, "See the dumpster,
parked on the street, I threw my wedding ring
into it."

I am left loving you as only a mother can.

Carolyn S. Nevin
Southside, AL

Christmas Trees

New Year's morning, I lay in bed thinking about taking down the Christmas tree. School was starting again tomorrow with a new set of teenagers entering my classroom each period. Today was the last free day I would have for a while.

Since it was always my mother who would so carefully remove each ornament and tenderly wrap it in tissue paper to store for next year, her absence this year was especially painful. I prayed I would be able to perform this task with a fraction of the love and care Mom always put into it. Since it was also the first Christmas without her in our lives, I also prayed not to shed too many tears.

I forced myself to get up and dress. I headed for the coffee pot and carried a cup over to the Christmas tree. The first decoration I noticed was one that had belonged to Mom. It was the only one left of her cherished set from the 1940s. In those days, all the glass decorations were quite delicate. They had a silvery background with subdued hues of pink, light blue, or violet. Most were round like the one I held in my hand and had three or four bands around their middles made of some scratchy white substance meant to resemble snow.

As I tried to remember the appearance of the other ornaments in that old set, I was suddenly a child again living in our home in Pennsylvania. It was one of those very lean years after Mom had to give up on trying to operate the TV business our father had left her with, complete with his unpaid debts. In the early 1950s, men often had little respect for a woman boss, and some of her repairmen began to steal from her. Mom had been trying to get a job for months. Having been an executive secretary before she married, those were the jobs she looked for in the newspaper. She answered every ad but was told each time that she was too old.

Carolyn S. Nevin
Southside, AL

We had been on public assistance for a while—it is called welfare now—and Mom hated having to accept what she considered to be charity. Our paternal grandfather helped by going to the distribution facility to stand in line for our ration of powdered eggs, peanut butter, and whatever else was available to poor people in any given week, because we no longer had a car.

He was a sweet man but a terrible driver, and he was quite ashamed of how his elder son had deserted us. My sister Maggie and I called him "Puppy." He lived in a rooming house in a nearby town, our grandmother having thrown him out of the house years before.

Our grandmother took our father's side, claiming that taking care of a family was too much responsibility for her poor boy. My father was forty-three years old when he left—hardly a boy. But he was inexperienced with women and fell for the wife of the owner of the restaurant next to his original shop, where he ate lunch every day. The woman was worldly and clever. She wanted out of her own childless marriage to an obese man who wore his cook's apron over dirty white undershirts and smoked big smelly cigars. She hatched a plan that the two couples would sell their businesses and move to Florida. They sold the restaurant first and moved. Then our father sold the shop next to the restaurant and kept the newer shop that was closer to our house to return and sell later. Once my father joined his lover in Florida, they planned to run off together. It was a clever plan, because leaving the state made it impossible for my mother to get any kind of child support for Maggie and me.

Our situation had worsened each year, and there was no end in sight, especially this year. Now it was Christmas Eve, and according to our family tradition, this was the day we were to put up and decorate a Christmas tree. But this year there was no money for a tree. Mom, Maggie, and I sullenly talked about this dilemma, wondering how in the world we could get a tree to put up in our empty dining room.

Carolyn S. Nevin
Southside, AL

The room was empty, because right before our father left, he convinced Mom to sell the dining room set for traveling money. He assured her we could get another set in Florida. The dining room remained empty from that day when men came to take away our furniture. Almost immediately after he had the money in hand, our father announced that he and the other couple would go ahead and fly to Florida. He would send for us when he found a place for us to live.

I still have the black and white pictures taken at the airport the day the three of them left. The woman must have been taking the photos. There is one with the unsuspecting husband actually dressed in a suit and tie. Then there is one of the four of us, Mom, sitting between Maggie and me, all three of us in our best dresses, Maggie and I with our hair in pony tails. My dad stood in his suit and tie behind Mom with his hands on her shoulders, as if holding her down. She was not looking at the camera and was not smiling.

"Mom is there no way we can find a Christmas tree?" I asked. "Aren't there trees in the woods?"

"Yes," Maggie agreed. "Maybe we could just find some branches to decorate and hang up over the mantle."

Mom looked from one of our worried faces to the other. She was silent for the next few minutes.

"I have an idea," she said. "Get bundled up—coats, hats, boots, gloves—and follow me!"

"In my mind's eye, I see our little troupe of three girls— well, Mom was forty-six—but Maggie was nine and I was eleven. We three trudged down the snow-covered hill that was our back yard all the way to the end of the property—a good five hundred feet from the house and nearly to the streetcar line. Our father had planted a row of four pine trees back in the day when he still cared about us. I think he planted them in the hopes that they would block the view of the streetcar tracks and the neighborhood on the other side.

Before he left, Dad was constantly working on that back yard. He built a wide path that zig-zagged back and forth

Carolyn S. Nevin
Southside, AL

across the hilly part of the yard. Then where the ground flattened out, he put a tire swing so high up in a giant chestnut tree that it swung back and forth across the entire width of the yard. It must have made a hundred-foot arc. We thought he was quite the acrobat to have climbed so high to tie the heavy rope in that enormous tree. He also built a huge fire pit and some picnic tables. He even wired the yard so that he could plug in his radio while he swung in his hammock in the shade on nice afternoons.

The neighborhood was made up of couples with small children. The adults liked to party on Saturday nights, and our back yard was a favorite spot. They would put the children to bed and gather in our back yard for a cookout. They made so much noise they woke me up sometimes. I remember being maybe four years old, tip-toeing across the hall to spy on them through the small window at the top of the stairs. They were drinking what I now know was beer from one of those old-fashioned kegs that was a big white square box with a spigot. The box was positioned at the edge of one of the picnic tables. It was the year before Dad left, and I remember gathering the neighborhood kids together the day after one of those parties to check if there was anything left in that big white box. There was, and it tasted awful.

Mom carried a saw and a hatchet and kept chattering cheerfully about how we would have a Christmas tree after all. None of us seemed to notice the bitter cold or realized how far we had walked.

Suddenly we all stopped, speechless, our gaze drawn upward to the tops of four huge pine trees. They had grown incredibly fast in the past few years and were way over even Mom's head. In fact, they were all more than twice as tall as her five-foot-five-inch frame.

Maggie and I exchanged worried looks.

"Okay," Mom said. "I guess we'll just have to cut off the top of one of these."

"How in the world will we do that?" I asked. "We can't

Carolyn S. Nevin
Southside, AL

even reach the lowest branch of one of them."

Mom was undeterred. "Here, this one," she said.

"You two can give me a boost."

"What?" Maggie said.

"Here," Mom grabbed our arms and reminded us how to make a kind of basket for carrying someone. "I can stand on your arms instead of sitting."

"Mom, I'm not sure this is safe," I said.

"Oh, I'll be okay," Mom said. "Remember how scared you two were when I painted the gutters on the back of the house? It was three stories up, and I made it without falling off the ladder. After that, this will be a piece of cake!"

Oh, yes, I remembered how each day she climbed that ladder, I was scared she might fall and make us orphans. The memory of that made the familiar churning in my gut begin.

Maggie and I obeyed and boosted Mom up to the lowest branch of the tree. She stood there for a few moments getting her bearings.

"I'll have to climb a little higher," she said. "The trunk is still too thick here."

With that Mom slowly worked her way up through the prickly branches until all we could see were the bottoms of her black boots. We gasped in unison.

"Okay, I'm going to start sawing. You two get out of the way. The place where I am cutting is about three inches thick, so it might take me a while." With that she went to work. But it was slow going—she was not used to handling the big saw. She took the hatchet out of a deep coat pocket and chopped off a few scraggly branches. As they fell to the ground, they gave off a distinct smell of resin. I picked up a branch and saw the roughness of it, imagining how scratchy it would feel against our skin. I hoped Mom still was wearing her gloves.

All of a sudden Mom yelled, "Timber!"

Maggie and I scrambled away in the opposite direction as

Carolyn S. Nevin
Southside, AL

the top of the tree crashed to the ground.

"Mom, please come down now. And be careful," I said.

She reached the lowest branch and could not decide what to do next.

"I'll sit down on this branch, and you two try to grab my legs and lower me down," she finally said.

We grabbed onto her legs but lost control of the rest of her partway down, and all three of us landed in a drift of soft snow. Nervous laughter ensued as we made sure no one was hurt.

Cutting off the top of that tree turned out to be the easy part. Over the next hour the three of us dragged, pushed, and pulled that treetop up the hill, up the driveway, and to the front yard, our cheeks glowing crimson from the cold by now. We just barely squeezed it through the front door, the treetop objecting the entire time.

Mom had the stand ready. She worked some magic, I think, getting those big screws into the trunk evenly. We stood the treetop up in the dining room and brushed the prickly debris off ourselves as well as we could.

There was suddenly complete silence as we three sat on the floor, exhausted, staring at what was supposed to be our Christmas tree. It did not look like a Christmas tree at all. Its branches were spindly and the needles were too long. The treetop was nearly as wide as it was tall. If we pushed it a bit off-center from the windows, we had a little room to walk past it to get to the kitchen—just barely. What a disaster!

Then suddenly Mom started giggling. It was infectious. Soon the three of us were rolling on the floor over stray pine needles laughing uncontrollably. Thank God for Mom's sense of humor. It always allowed us to practically sail through those really bad times. I can still hear her saying, "Remember, necessity is the mother of invention."

Mom brought out a small carton of ornaments she had been saving since the 1940s. She also had a few strings of old-fashioned lights. The bulbs were bigger than those on the

Carolyn S. Nevin
Southside, AL

chandelier in my present dining room, and they only came in red, blue, green, and orange. We put what we had on the tree. Then Mom gingerly unwrapped a small paper bag of silver icicles. She had taken them off last year's tree one at a time and kept them. We added those and pronounced our tree to be beautiful. Now it really was Christmas!

The neighborhood kids came over to play during Christmas vacation and mostly made fun of our tree. But we three girls grew to love it dearly by the time it came down on Epiphany. And as it turns out, it is the only Christmas tree from my childhood that I remember.

I am taking ornaments one by one and putting them on the coffee table to be wrapped, just like Mom used to do. I'm finding some of Mom's ornaments from later years, after she and my father got married again. How is that for a family story? They were married for ten years, divorced for seventeen, then married again to each other for a little over six years. And I remember that New Year's Day is the day my father drowned in a sailing accident and left my mother for a second time. A few years later she came to live with us and took over as caretaker of the Christmas tree. My husband Tom and I had wanted to give Mom a place to live out her last years, which we thought were already upon her. Besides, she was the only grandparent our son Daniel would have the chance to know. But Mom fooled us and lived with us for twenty more years, helping us to build lasting traditions.

Today I decide I'm not going to be sad. The ornaments on the tree are all so special. They remind me of good times gone by. There are ornaments that Tom and Daniel each made when they were in kindergarten. Then there is our son's first Christmas ornament, ornaments from trips, and gifts from students and friends. And there is the collection of Hallmark ornaments Mom gave Daniel each year for about twelve years. All of these are a reminder of my special mom and how much she loved Christmas, especially the trees. Without a tree, it just wasn't Christmas.

Robert Erickson
Round Pond, ME

Winter

My mind peers out on ultimate grey
If snow and cold could talk, they'd say
"This is winter, so cold and bleak
With wind and slush; misery I speak"

Peering again on the harbor round
Grey ocean to grey shore out to the sound
My frigid soul cries out in abject thirst
For the soothing warmth of an August First

***

Years Missed

All the years I worked and toiled.
All the years living life embroiled.
The saddest of those that are on the list,
Are all the years with you I missed.

Sally Belenardo
Branford, CT

Garden Clothes

Dressed in dainty
Dutchman's breeches

fastened with
bachelor buttons

and wearing some
hand-picked

accessories
such as foxgloves,

lady slippers,
and a Turk's cap lily,

indeed you have
elegant taste—

but with no garment
from neck to waist,

while the sun wraps
himself in clouds,

don't be surprised
if you're chilly.

the late Anne W. Hammond
Woolwich, ME

South Branch Tote Road

Peace is a spell of random fortune:
No motion, no movement on the logging road.

It might be the grass or July flowers at peak,
Or the sun which stuns at ninety five degrees,

Or the shelter of greens which radiate fresh air,
Or the wind withheld by the forest trees...

In the tote road, the fortune breaks:
A mourning cloak smites the earth,

Flashes purple wings and yellow stripes, and waits.
Satyrs and big-eyed wood nymphs sweep

Out of the woods, swarm roadside grasses.
A mob of fritillaries splash silver spots,

Soak up sun with beating wings, or race down
The road at java speed to avoid a murdering bird.

A lemon sulfur rips by with zig zag, flight-line twists;
Hard for a dragon fly to seize her and make a feast.

A comma flutters in mud, sips hidden nutrients,
Refuses to move at the tread of a boot or close camera clicks.

Drawn by the smell, a silvery blue attacks a sneaker.
Salt brings a rusty comma to land

Beside the shining jewel,
Her tongue lightly lips the trousers.

In the still of the forest, no creature breathes.
Peace is a spell of random fortune.

Janice Babcock
Wauwatosa, WI

Good Samaritan

Dragging my lawn mower from its tomb under the porch. It awaits transport. On my deserted dead end street, no help in sight. My sidekick for 51 years has an appointment. This vintage machine is dented and rusty. The saving grace is the original owner's manual with all its parts. The lawnmower store wants to display it.

I struggle unsuccessfully to load the mower into my car. A truck randomly drives down my street. My Good Samaritan has arrived. The driver lifts this relic into my trunk. Its final ride is a place of honor.

***

Thomas Peter Bennett
Silver Spring, MD

Autumn Hold Out

A stately green aspen
And a disrobing yellow maple,
Framed brownish oaks with
Dry leaves still clinging.

As the days shorten,
Five yellow leaves
Cling to a knotty branch
On the nude maple.

They quiver, glistening golden
In late autumn's morning light,
Resisting winter's fate.

Stanley Robinson
Bridgewater, NJ

Marriage

Three score plus four years ago
We gave each other in union
At the time there was no way to know
Is this a proper communion

All we knew was our intuition
That this seemed correct for us
Would this arrangement develop fruition
The thought wasn't worth the fuss

Our decision came from the heart
Nothing else seemed to matter
Devine guidance was there from the start
Thank heaven for the latter

As years passed by our dependency
Our bond became much stronger
Our major search was what shall we do
To make all this last longer

You must also eliminate conflict
It's a serious danger zone
Disparate values you must restrict
Remember you're not alone

Talk to each other to understand
Each other's needs are important
Reach out a friendly helping hand
And harmony will be the resultant

Stanley Robinson
Bridgewater, NJ

So here we are three score and plus
With a vow we never forget
There is nothing more important to us
Then the days that have passed since we met

***

Frances Henkel
Wauwatosa, WI

Hidden

Trees
of summer
clad
in leaves
uncountable,
bear gifts
of beauty
and mystery.
Not until
their season
of color
passes
and limbs
are barren
do we see
the secret
surprise
of the
nest
that
harbored
the songs
of summer.

Thomas Peter Bennett
Silver Spring, MD

Autumn Aerobatics

A silhouette against the November sky
On a tall oak's highest bare branches,
A ten foot leap…
    Down,
        Down,
Onto a scraggly branch in a nearby oak.

A lateral short jump to an aspen's branch,
Then a fast dive…
    Down,
        Twenty feet down,
And a snag on a low-hanging branch.

A floating hop…
    Down,
        Down,
To acorn laden leaves,
A squirrel's snack on Thanksgiving Day.

***

Crow Winter

The last clinging leaves are gone,
The maple stands bare,
Except for three ebony crows
Preening in the sunset,
As the winter wind
Rocks the nude branches
They are gripping.

Eduardo Jiménez Mayo
San Antonio, TX

Coffee Pond

In Maine there is a wooded lake called Coffee Pond, where our maternal cousins and we used to summer in a log cabin after quite a drive. Our point of origin was Andover, Massachusetts, home to a famous college preparatory school that resembles a college more than a high school in facilities, faculty, expanse and expense. In passing through New Hampshire, we used to make a detour along a highway called Kancamagus for wading in the nearby waterfalls. You can find these places easily enough on your GPS, which is why I haven't bothered to detail them here.

Coincident to the trip were guaranteed indulgences in submarine sandwiches, most often at a diner called Amato's. I remember my siblings and cousins devouring exponential combinations of baguettes, cold cuts, salads, cheeses and olive oil, though I preferred meatballs and marinara sauce on mine. A curious detail about Amato's was that in the lobby there was a treasure chest filled with assorted trinkets and small toys, where we would grab what we could on our way out the door. Since the rise of fast food chains specializing in the sub, there isn't much room left for expounding on the subject, except to emphasize the quality of the Maine subs over the relatively stale ones that migrated to my father's hometown of San Antonio, where I was raised and continue to live.

Ogunquit lobsters came in second place, as far as we concerned ourselves with culinary matters. A shallow pool outside our favorite restaurant provided dubious shelter to scores of those non-kosher creatures averaging three pounds or more. Years later I read an apocryphal story about how Salvador Dalí used to walk his pet lobster up and down the streets of New York City to the astonishment of the tourists and the annoyance of the natives. What I do know is that

Eduardo Jiménez Mayo
San Antonio, TX

Harvard University hosts a lobster bake each year for its freshman class, at least it did in 1995, and my Jewish roommate taught me a lesson in comparative religion by bestowing his ticket upon me in disgust at the thought of having to ingest one of those unholy one-pounders on display for our dining pleasure.

Having attended Catholic schools in San Antonio throughout my childhood and perhaps because the Jewish population here, though impressive, is relatively small, I can't say that I was ever close to any Jewish boys or girls growing up. At Coffee Pond, however, there was a Jewish family at the end of the lake: Mr. and Mrs. Stoll and their children. I hardly knew what it meant to be Jewish at the time but I do remember a sense of "difference," you might say, separating us from them.

Their motorboat was hopelessly outdated, I remember that, and it was canopied whereas ours was topless, and they rarely ventured past the cove where they lived. "The Stolls stole the boat! The Stolls stole the boat!" I remember that refrain erupting when we naughty children awoke one morning to find our boat missing from the raft at which we docked it. Later that morning a few suntanned all-Americans from the boys' camp on the far side of the lake tugged it back to us in their canoe, having found it adrift.

One day on Coffee Pond was about the same as the next, but the day my older sister and my Madonna-look-alike cousin flew in an Air Force transport helicopter was eventful from the start. A few of the younger children, myself included, had been ordered to the spring to fetch water. Our only consolation was that we were also able on such occasions to pick berries along the way, even if it meant wandering off into the woods without parental authorization. The fruits of our labor would be incorporated into the breakfast menu with no questions asked.

We satiated our puerile appetites that morning on blueberry, strawberry and blackberry pancakes expertly grilled at

Eduardo Jiménez Mayo
San Antonio, TX

the hands of my uncle with the widest girth. Chores came next. We picked those blindly from a baseball cap, though I always seemed to get the latrine. I became quite the expert in toilets over time, and to this day I can unstop just about any toilet, anywhere, any time, by any available means. Luckily by the time our families bought that ailing cabin, which would have been in the early eighties, the outhouse had moved indoors.

My older sister interrupted my aunts, uncles and parents engaged in an intense match of cribbage. It must have been past noontime because the gin and tonic had already over-taken the card players' minds. I hadn't slept well the night before, incidentally. Up in the loft, surrounded by the youngest cousins, my peers, I dreamed that I had walked in my sleep onto the rafters and was to be rescued by an angel whose wings had been clipped by God for disobedience.

Next I dreamed that I was awake but I couldn't get up. Sensing that I would die in my sleep, I forced myself out of that trance into daylight. No one else was in the loft at that time, so I allowed myself to cry a little. I had forgotten all about my nightmares after hauling water from the spring, eating breakfast, and doing my chores. But when I saw my older sister crying, the memory of my own tears came rush-ing back.

My Madonna-look-alike cousin remained on the phone with Loring Air Force Base under firm orders not to hang up. She and my older sister had wanted to ride a train into Boston, and had looked up the number to the scheduling office in a dusty old phonebook that the previous owners of the cabin had left behind. Apparently, the number they dialed put them in touch with missile defense systems at Loring Air Force Base. It was rumored that there were nuclear missiles housed there, on guard against the Russians. Who had given them the secret number? Who were these girls?

Names, dates of birth, drivers' licenses, social security

Eduardo Jiménez Mayo
San Antonio, TX

numbers: in a matter of minutes the Air Force had conduct-
ed background checks on our families and were asking to
speak to the parents. My mother, perhaps the only sober one
at table, went to the living room and took up the only phone
in the cabin, thinking it surely was some kind of joke. My
older sister and cousin stood by. Meanwhile, the game in the
dining room was suspended.

When my mother reentered the dining room, crying her-
self, everyone at table realized it wasn't a joke and there was
no more cribbage played that afternoon. My uncle with the
widest girth, trying his best not to slur his speech, took up
the telephone next. The atmosphere was tenser than the
cribbage game had been at its height. All the adults and chil-
dren came over to lend moral support, if nothing else. To the
military's credit, it quickly realized that it was dealing with a
bunch of nobodies: a few inebriated cribbage players and
their unsophisticated children, none of them with Russian
alliances, and the women's tears began to dry up.

The commanding officer offered to send a transport heli-
copter to escort the young ladies to Boston, and he would not
listen to my uncle's attempts at discouragement. The "open-
ing," as we called it, a large clearing in the woods immediate-
ly across the lake from our cabin, was selected for the land-
ing spot. The aircraft arrived and whisked away the teenage
girls to a restricted landing site near Boston. Against the
wonder of it all they were instructed not to speak of the trip.
To their credit they never did reveal their experiences in the
air, except for a comment or two about how handsome were
the crewmen.

Robert Hodum
Sound Beach, NY

Dusk Coming On

Stalks of corn ablaze
With the scent of burned pumpkin rind,

Knotted smoke of maple leaves
Teased up by a silver wind,
From this afternoon's pyre,
Mounded high.

Beads of molten hickory and spruce
Roll down the glint
Of autumn's smoldering twilight,

Rounded orange shapes
Call anxiously
From their core's
Dangling strings and seed.

Their evening's chorus
Accompanies the cinnabar horizon,
As light shrinks back
From the ripeness of this October eve

Lorelee Sienkowski
Packwaukee, WI

Have a Nice Day

"Have a nice day," the dead-planner said
After scheming my final repose:
No flowers, no tufting, no casket at all,
Just ashes and vessel I chose.

I want a coffee can, either Folgers or Max,
Not one of those generic brands
And a site on a hill with a tree at the plot,
God willing, and all goes to plan.

In the meantime, I'm living and learning,
Pretending each day is my last.
I care for my captives, domestic and wild,
And find joy in each healthy repast.

I hope when I'm nothing but ashes
Composting to dirt and to clay
That my family remembers with laughter
That I showed them to live for each day.

Maxine Weintraub
Wayland, MA

Early One Spring Morning

It was just too early to be so wide awake. The sun was barely lighting up the sky over the ocean, and there I was, up for the day. A nightgown and a thin robe kept me comfortable in the chilly Maine spring morning as I left my bedroom and walked out on to the front porch to see if the newspaper—by some miracle—had arrived.

No miracle, so I went around to the back of the house to check on the progress of the perennial garden. The daylilies were short, pale green spikes and the ladies' mantle was about the size of a small teacup. I loved that ladies' mantle. She could be found sometimes as early as February, peeking her way up out of ground that was still snow covered. I would give her a gentle pat, a soft hello and welcome back, so glad to see her after the dark Maine winter.

A slight stirring to my left caught my attention. There, less than ten feet away was a mid-sized doe, warming herself in the pale sunlight. Deer were everywhere at dawn and sunset, feasting on our evergreens, waiting for just the perfect moment to breakfast on opening tulip bulbs. And usually these skittish animals bounded off gracefully at the slightest movement.

Not this doe. She held her ground. Remained. I did not move for some moments, then slowly and carefully dared to look her straight in the eye. She took that dare and returned my gaze. She did not move. And so we stayed. Finally, the doe shook her head slightly, flicked a perky ear in a kind of social acknowledgement, then turned her back to me, flashed her white tail, and slowly sauntered off into the surrounding woods, leaving me shaken and alone in the morning sun.

Mary Jo Balistreri
Waukesha, WI

Layered in Winter
Washington Park, Milwaukee, WI

I
Muffled in mittens, snowsuits and scarfs,
with skates tied and flung over shoulders,
we headed for the neighborhood rink—
smoke, pine, ozone-fresh air.

By the time the swirling smell of hot chocolate and music
from the loud speaker reached us, we were belting out
Wake Up Little Susie right along with the Everly Brothers.

Snippets of chatter and laughter swallowed our voices
as we elbowed our way through the crowd of kids
going to, coming from the warming house. The potbelly stove
tossed a blast of heat at the cold we carried.

On long narrow benches, we squeezed together, bodies bent
nearly double. We peeled off boots and tightened laces,
were already dashes of sliver speeding across ice.

We'd play *crack the whip* or *I send*, show off, skate
backward or spin one-legged arabesques,
ice chips and crusts of snow flying when we missed
and slid on our bottoms.

Risk was everything.

II
As we grew older, Washington Park was a fever—
Friday night dates, moonlight and lanterns, *Skaters Waltz*,
Chances are, and *Don't forbid me.*
It was holding hands, arms around each other,

(continued)

Mary Jo Balistreri
Waukesha, WI

that first trembling kiss.

Years later, Elvis is wood smoke, and wet wool,
a cold sweep of winter that unlatches
memory's trunk.

Lost parts of us glide near, and we reclaim
silver blades under stars, images of runes etched
on ice, our first love raised from the dead,
the kiss ever moist on our lips.

We were the air, and everything,
everything was possible.

***

Behind the Curtain

Grief is a mosaic, the glass leaking light
where the edges don't fit. She tries to glue between
the panes, but in her fluid world everything bends and
     curves away.

She is here and then she isn't—the morphine drip
releasing her to the dark belly of memory:
     a red airplane sweater, wind filling its empty arms
          on the clothesline,
     a library card slipping from a boy's striped shirt,
          the struggle to retrieve it.

Sometimes, she hears the older boy say *checkmate*,
his voice fading like the echo of a finale.

Holding my daughter, I stroke her hair, this grown woman
made small again.

Susan Gerry
Friendship, ME

Carnival Mirrors

Memory can trick you.
Change things around. Fuzz out the edges
until you aren't quite sure what happened anymore
or how you feel about it.

But the past is always present,
It swirls beneath the surface
distorted, as by carnival mirrors,
until we can bear to remember.

***

Robert Hodum
Sound Beach, NY

Night Walk

Pilgrims' peace of St. James,
Swallows' flight unseen
In the light of a pale moon passing,
Let fall
Life's stones of blame, guilt
And years of disbelief,
Along this road that pulls us forward.
Leave angry words,
Mistrust,
And yearnings ill conceived
In the shadows
Along the Way this eve,
And find pilgrims' peace in Santiago.

Jean Lawrence
Waldoboro, ME

Bumblebees and Bobby

If you're as old as I am, you probably remember the biased verses that were bantered about in our youth: "Sugar and spice and everything nice—that's what little girls are made of!" "Snakes and snails and puppy dog tails—that's what little boys are made of!" While I didn't believe the words or take them literally, the difference between boys and girls was very clearly impressed on me in my early years, especially when it came to playtime activities. I can firmly attest that I was never a Tom Boy; I left that up to my younger sister! My mother's admonition: "Be a good girl" was taken to heart, for the most part. I really tried to please my parents. However, everyone slips up now and then, and a slip can demonstrate that being a good girl all the time really isn't much fun!

It was a warm early July afternoon in 1947. I had finished my lunch and taken the dishes to the sink while my mother settled my younger sister for her afternoon nap. Mom knew that I was going to walk down to my friend Genevieve's house, for I had told her that we planned to play dolls or school outside in the yard. I had promised to help Genevieve bring her stuff to my yard right after lunch.

As I started down the sidewalk, I noticed that all was very quiet on the street. Curtains were drawn to protect from the heat of the sun and there was a feeling of lethargy in the air. I slowed my walk as I got closer to Bobby Healey's house two doors down, when his sister June, who was in high school, came rushing out the door and jumped on the back of her boyfriend's motorcycle. In a cloud of exhaust and a loud roar of the engine which pierced the quiet of the street, they took off.

Now what I observed was not an unusual sight, for June was, in the words of many of the adults on the street, "a lively

Jean Lawrence
Waldoboro, ME

one." For me, she was quite impressive. She had lovely red hair, wore a leather jacket whenever she got on the back of the bike, was the drum majorette in the high school band, had a baton and the greatest pair of white leather boots with tassels that I had ever seen in a parade. She was the kind of girl that a seven year old dreamed of becoming despite what some adults might think or say.

As June and her guy zoomed down the road, I continued my walk to Genevieve's. The house was all closed up and not a soul seemed to be around. "Could she have forgotten our plans?" I wondered as I knocked on the door. Receiving no answer, I walked around out back and tried the kitchen door. No luck!

Now it just happened that many of the backyards of the houses on my street connected with one another, and in those days, no one fenced in his property. So, I decided to walk home through the backyards instead of going back to the sidewalk. This is where my afternoon's fun as well as trouble began.

In order to return to my yard, I had to go through three other yards, one of which was Bobby Healey's. Now, just as his sister intrigued me, Bobby intrigued all the kids in the area even more. He was about four years older than we, that alone was a big plus, but he had the most beautiful red Schwinn two wheeled bike in town! It was always stationed just outside his back door during the day, and he washed and simonized it regularly while many of us "kids" looked on admiringly. Bobby's prowess with the bike was also enviable, for he could peddle it with great energy and wheel it about and send gravel all over the playground. And when with clothes pins he attached playing cards to the front and back wheels, his bike sounded just like a motorbike. How he loved showing off, and how every kid on the street envied him!

Now, most of the mothers in the neighborhood expressed some concern about Bobby's bike actions, but it wasn't until his dad helped him put up a pup tent in the backyard, that

Jean Lawrence
Waldoboro, ME

the mothers started their litany. It went something like this: "Under no circumstances are you to go in Bobby Healey's tent. Don't go near Bobby Healey's tent! Stay away from Bobby Healey's tent!!!" I was very familiar with this warning, for my mother had recited it to me often especially when Genevieve and I traipsed through the backyards from my house to hers.

Instead of heading for home by avoiding the tent and walking way around it, I really didn't think much about my mother. As I neared Bobby's tent, there in the tent's opening was a wooden case that caught my eye. I edged nearer and discovered Bobby bent over the case.

"What 'ya doing, Bobby?" I asked.

"Experimenting," he replied.

"Can I watch? Can I help?"

My questions seemed to tumble out of my mouth before I could catch them.

"I suppose so if you're quiet," was his reply.

I was immediately mesmerized and willingly sank to the ground. As I hunkered down just outside the tent opening, I learned that the case held a junior chemistry set made up of a magnifying glass, tweezers, and all kinds of vials, bottles, and glass slides. It had a small tripod on which Bobby had attached a flat piece of shingle, so he had a table on which to carry out his activities. I was captivated by the actions that he pursued. He proceeded to put bumblebees in vials and shake them vigorously until they seemed drunk; next he took another bee, put it in a vial with dirt and shook it until it passed out or died; I didn't ask which. He tried to find a bee's stinger and remove it. He sent me off with a jar to get him some more bees from the clover patch nearby and then pro-ceeded to fry bees using his magnifying glass and the rays of the sun. I was so taken with Bobby's control of his experi-ments and his few but vivid comments to his victims that I really became at one with what was going on before me. Over and over in my head, I kept saying, "We're 'sperimenting;

Jean Lawrence
Waldoboro, ME

we're 'sperimenting!"

I didn't have any idea of how much time had elapsed since leaving home and might have gotten away with my extra-curricular activity if my mother had not decided to venture into the backyard to take in her wash and realized that we girls were not there. All of a sudden, out of the blue came my mother's voice, "Jean, get yourself home!"

Well, didn't I jump up and start for home as fast as my legs would carry me. To my surprise and embarrassment, my mother appeared just as I rounded the corner and started up the steps. Her hand met with my posterior and assisted me into the house. Each assist she gave me as I mounted the stairs to my bedroom was accented with, "I told you to stay away from Bobby Healey's tent!" Believe me, though my feelings were hurt more than my bottom, I assured her, through my howls, that I was sorry.

"You will stay in your bedroom until supper time, and then we'll talk over your actions with your father!" were her words of reply.

As I sat in my bedroom and contemplated my afternoon foray into the world of experiments with the captivating Bobby Healey, I came to realize that if I squeezed myself way to the right side of the window of my bedroom, I could see the tent which had held such exciting moments this afternoon. Can you believe it? Bobby was still there!

During the next few hours, I never gave a thought to my mother's warning regarding the impending "talk" with Dad. Instead, what kept ringing in my head were the words of Bobby's prediction, "Tomorrow, worms!"

David Campbell
Somerville, MA

Honfleur Harbor 1864
Watercolor by J.B. Jongkind, Fogg Museum

One glance and I am beside him
at the water's edge, seeing what he sees.
He is 45, I am 33, as happy to be here
while he paints as to paint myself.

The Channel sky shreds itself
and threatens the land. It excites us,
it is why we are here,
it is why we know each other.

It makes him lay down washes
like a man giving first aid, a man
who will not have access to paint
for the rest of his life.

A blue-grey knob lunging in
from the right-hand horizon spits cold rain
and plants ghostly polka dots
in the wet bands across his sky.

He swears, but we know it hardly matters.
Like getting cold and wet ourselves,
it is part of being here.
Being here is the main thing.

Jim Mello
Brewer, ME

Awakenings: Post Op

still under the spell
of sedative induced Nirvana

just this side of impairment
he blesses himself

with childhood inculcated ritual

forehead, heart, scapulas
touched

by moving fingers
slicing the air with remembered symbols

warmed with the embers of memory
inflamed with thanksgiving for the sacrament of
the next breath

***

Patrick T. Randolph
Lincoln, NE

The Power of Observation

Garden light—
        fireflies find a home inside
        an old Jack-o-lantern's
               watchful eyes.

Zibette Dean
Edgecomb, ME

Mudflats

She's twelve, tall and blonde.
The tide's out
but we go
to the cove anyway
wade the sandy brookbed
hunt for shells
and clams' squirtholes.

The clay flats are squishy
mucky, slippery.
She skates barefoot
on the mud
then clothes herself in mud.

Long black gloves
long black stockings;
she poses like a twelve-year-old starlet
then pelts me with mud, laughing.

Sally Woolf-Wade
New Harbor, ME

Minstrel

He wakes, perspiring, from a dream,
stretched out at back of lurching bus,
his guitar pressed against his chest.
His fingers linger on the frets,
desperate to continue, but
scraps and bills spread out beside him.
No time to make the music,
no space to pull the lyrics
from the clutter in his mind.
The traveling minstrel scribbles
words on shreds of paper napkins,
snatching minutes on the road,
mindful of the passing hours.
He knows the journey's nearly over.
Evening glow will soon be gone.
He hopes, before the dark will rise,
there might be time for one more song.

Kathy McHugh
Ogunquit, ME

Eulogy for Dad

When we were young Dad said to my brother Mark, "I'm not going to be the type of father to be playing ball with you out in the yard." What Dad did for Mark was actually better; for Mark learned so much from Dad over the years that he, like Dad, can fix or do just about anything: mechanical, technical, electrical, automotive, computers, carpentry, masonry and plumbing. Together Dad's and Mark's efforts solved and saved so much for our family, but mostly they enjoyed the camaraderie of it.

Manchester native Mom met Dad, the officer from western NY, at a local St. Anselm event. They were married on November 18, 1944 in Boise, Idaho. After the war they moved to the second floor of 524 Merrimack Street, then next door to my grandparents at 1235 Island Pond Road, the second of twelve homes Mom and Dad would acquire over the course of their 70 years together.

Not being able to bear children, Mom and Dad decided to adopt, and fortunately through the Catholic Charities organization they found Mark, an active young toddler whom three or four families had previously taken in but returned. This time Mark stayed for good. This was meant to be. This was home.

Two years later they adopted me, an infant born in Peterborough. At 18 months I was admitted to the Sacred Heart Hospital with spinal meningitis and was given last rites, destined to die until prayers and penicillin turned things around and saved my life. I remember skating on a frozen lake with Mom and Dad on either side of me, holding my hands while I watched other kids attempting to skate, falling yet uninjured due to padded snow suits. My parents wanted to protect me then, but later on they gave me the gift of a university education both as a writer and caregiver—

Kathy McHugh
Ogunquit, ME

both which I was destined to become.

1968 was a not so good year. Walt Disney died. Robert F. Kennedy and Martin Luther King were shot. The telephone workers went on strike. Dad the manager worked many hours to maintain telephone service for customers from the seacoast to the lakes region of New Hampshire, including Sanbornville and Wolfeboro. I missed him a lot that year. Wolfeboro is where I spent a few summer weeks at Camp Bernadette on Lake Wentworth. One day I was in the activity building gluing beads on paper and looked up to see a familiar army green telephone company car slowly driving by toward the main road. It was Dad! I wanted so much to run out there to greet him, to get him to turn around and come back, but knew I had to stay where I was. I knew I'd see him soon.

So what is a father? To me it means tour guide, hero, pilot, role model, leader, manager, mentor, advisor and best friend—strong and tall. Some claim that Dad might have trouble with the paternal role as his father deserted his mother back in the 1920s/early 1930s. However, Dad succeeded from CC Camp to the military to New England Telephone where he worked for 35 years. Some criticize his not being a churchgoer, yet Bill Ott had a most generous heart. He was a thoughtful considerate gentleman; a supreme example of kindness and second chances.

"He was tough yet fair," a former employee of Dad's told me when I worked for Ma Bell for a few years myself. Workers who recognized that I'm Bill Ott's daughter treated me with respect. They missed working for Dad.

We can be sure that our Heavenly Father will welcome Dad into his kingdom, but along the way I'm certain that God will go on Skype and ask Dad if he'll look over his computer, install a program, fix his printer or teach him some Windows secrets.

Now Mom and Dad have found their thirteenth and eternal home together in heaven.

Kathy McHugh
Ogunquit, ME

There are so many things that just belong together: mustard and relish, peanut butter and jelly, bacon and eggs, hotdogs and beans, pancakes and syrup, sand and sea, Huntley and Brinkley—and of course Doris and Bill. One is just not right without the other, yet I've marveled at Dad's strength to go on after losing Mom and function so well, sticking to his daily routine at the age of 94.

Let me share with you what Dad loves and maybe you can also joyfully live into your 90's and beyond: Lobster, pecan pie, scotch and soda, coffee, salted butter, chicken noodle soup, eggs and bacon, crunchy peanut butter on English muffins, pretzels or ripple chips, reading the newspaper, watching the news, birds at the feeder and deer in the yard, completing jigsaw and word puzzles, connecting with friends via live computer networks and ham radio, wearing breathing strips at bedtime and listening to the radio all night.

The *Bible* says, "Honor thy mother and father." Television gave us *Father Knows Best, Make Room for Daddy, My Three Sons* and *Leave It To Beaver*. Shakespeare wrote, "Goodnight Sweet Prince," and I say, "Thanks, Dad, for everything and until we meet again I know that your love and all that you taught us will keep us strong today and in the days to come. I love you Dad."

Sylvia Little-Sweat
Wingate, NC

Encounter

Lines formed in the dark
before the closed flaps
of a tent where the steam
of coffee and hot chocolate
underway fogged the air.
Legs like paper straws sucked
the bitter cold despite feet
that tried to stamp it down.
After an hour I left the line
to lean against a winter tree
raising one leg to wick some
body heat. Bundled in coats
a black man approached me
and asked if he could share
my tree. *There's tree enough
for two*, I exclaimed through
wool wrapped loosely around
my nose and mouth. *I'd like
to sit but fear I cannot stand
again with feet so numb.* He
vowed to get me up. Like old
friends who share a courthouse
bench, we passed the time
and spoke of hope: children
educated; a nation changed.
Time takes change. . .
he mused—a slip of tongue
no doubt but nonetheless true
for he had lived in a South
where in darkest days to face
a white woman—day or night—

(continued)

Sylvia Little-Sweat
Wingate, NC

could have got him cut, jailed,
or hanged. But here we sat
on frozen ground beneath
a dormant tree. Extending
willing arms he took my
hands in his and lifted me.

***

Sherry B. Hanson
Portland, OR

Grand Pre, August 1999

They arrive in mid-summer
soaring and wheeling in unison
above the Minas Basin,
their cloud-piercing arabesques
making no sound.
Thousands of sandpipers
casing the flats at Evangeline Beach
for tiny brine shrimp
left in the sand.

No sound
until they close on the beach.
A whir of wings
as they drop
in front of the sun
to skitter at water's edge
feeding, resting finally,
asleep on their feet.

Robert Hodum
Sound Beach, NY

Pulling Tight

An arm-entwined
Skate of a dance
Beneath
Snow's waterfall,
Phantom ballerinas
Gliding jig
Down trolley tracks
Thru port's evening storm,
Melded two-headed
Lovers' chats
Crest and sink
At street-end's blur,
Glazed
Sloops and buoys,
Their cadence marked
By icy currents' thaw,
White-laced pilings
Hold fast
The tug *Carrie Mae*,
Close to shore.
As dawn's
Window dressings
Draw tight,
Against last night's Artic squall

Rebecca Recor
Round Pond, ME

had to admire his crafty tactic even as I pointed out that his vision wasn't the issue; it was that his processing of information had slowed down. Repeating this conversation over and over, I reminded myself not to let my voice rise or my frustration show. He couldn't remember the earlier times we had skirmished over the same ground. "You're taking away my independence. You're treating me like a child," he protested.

Rather than escalating the battle, I tried to show I understood where he was coming from. After all, this was the man who had jogged next to me as I wobbled down the driveway on my first two-wheeler and later had taught me how to parallel park. On the other hand, I had to stand firm about this decision for his safety and that of everyone else. To avoid outright conflict, I proposed, "Let's pretend we've already had the long drawn-out battle over your driving, and that I've won!" The blank look on his face probably resembled the one I had given him decades before when confronted with "Because I said so!" for the umpteenth time.

Sometimes the struggle took place without words. I confiscated both sets of his keys, but he located a third set while I was out of town and tried to move the car. Luckily, the battery was dead because the car had sat unused in the driveway for so many months. I conveniently neglected to get a new battery until late August when a visiting friend really needed to borrow the car.

In September I took Dad to renew his driver's license, thinking he could use it as an ID that didn't announce to the world that he could no longer drive. I checked the DMV notice carefully to make sure we had all the right documents. We even stopped at the bank to get his birth certificate out of the safe deposit box before driving down to Topsham. It was not until we arrived that I discovered he hadn't brought his new eyeglasses, or even his Reny's reading glasses, with him. As he squinted in frustration, I helped him fill out the forms. The clerk smiled sympathetically but said he couldn't give Dad a new license unless he came back with his glasses that

Rebecca Recor
Round Pond, ME

day or had the eye doctor pass on his vision. In the meantime we got him a state photo ID as a backup.

Four days later Dad received two important pieces of mail. The first was a letter from the DMV saying, "As it has come to our attention that Clifford has physical or mental issues that might interfere with his driving, a doctor's release will be required for him to receive a driver's license." Dr. Green had already decreed that Dad should not drive, (and, no, the optometrist could not complete this form), so it was final: Dad could no longer drive. A power higher than his daughter had spoken. I was privately thrilled that the State of Maine would protect the roads this way. Dad, of course, was devastated. The second item in the mail was a $700 bill to renew his auto insurance. It was relatively easy to convince my frugal father that shelling out big bucks to insure and register a car that was just going to sit in the driveway didn't make much sense. He agreed to get rid of his beloved car.

The Toyota Avalon was in great shape and had all the bells and whistles. It was six years old with only 19,000 miles on it. After all, it had sat in the driveway most of its life. It was more comfortable and in better shape than my SUV, but it wasn't the type of car I wanted. Just as we started wondering how to go about selling the car, fate stepped in. A friend of a friend emailed me to say the Avalon might be just the right car for him. We set up a time for him to check out the car on Friday. I spent seven hours preparing the car for its audition—driving it to Yudy's to be inspected, digging out all the official papers from old files, vacuuming the interior, polishing the glass inside and out, buffing the exterior. I felt like the Karate Kid as I repeated the circular motions until I thought my arm would fall off. I was just picking up the last paper towels in the driveway when John, the prospective buyer, arrived.

After a few minutes of introduction, John took the car for a test drive and returned to write Dad a check for $500 more

Rebecca Recor
Round Pond, ME

than I thought we would get. Before he dashed off to obtain the registration and insurance forms he would need to take possession of the car, I invited John and his wife to Dad's birthday party on Sunday. John drove off in his truck, and Dad and I looked at each other in amazement. In less than a week, Dad had not only reached the decision to sell his car but managed to do it. Of course that didn't count the months it took for Dad to accept the fact that he could no longer drive. *All in the fullness of time*, I thought. Putting my arm around Dad, I whispered, "I'm proud of you."

Two days later almost sixty people attended the open house to celebrate Dad's ninety-fifth birthday. He was the life of the party and enjoyed every minute: drinking martinis with the men, accepting kisses from the ladies, singing to recorded tunes of the thirties and forties, and glancing surreptitiously at each guest's name tag to have some idea whom he was addressing.

As the party wound down, John approached us, saying it was time for him to head back to Camden. Dad stared at him blankly, not making the connection; I went to get a large envelope with extra documents for the Toyota and all three sets of car keys. Realizing what an important moment it was, I grabbed my camera. No, I wasn't capturing the excitement of a sixteen year old blowing out her candles and being handed the keys to a bright red convertible; this was a ninety-five year old driving veteran, relinquishing his sword, giving up the symbol of his independence, and wondering what would go next. Dad's reluctance was palpable, but he finally dropped the keys into John's hand.

It struck me that the soundtrack for this scene was all wrong. Rather than the World War II songs still playing in the background or the rousing verses of Happy Birthday we'd been belting out a few minutes before, it should be something softer, more reflective, perhaps The Byrds harmonizing to their hit "To Everything There Is a Season. Turn. Turn. Turn." Or, even better, a muted bugle sounding "Taps."

Karen E. Wagner
Ashland, MA

Delayed Departures

Fog
slinks around corners
shaves edges dull,
spills over ground
erases feet,
blows over fingers
my hand is
shadowed
inches from my face,
sets me adrift.
I rock in a sea of
foam and gull screeches
my memory sets sail
for a port of pirates,
mates swing
from the highest yardarms,
treasures of the high seas
await the daring;
we sail with the tide
to chase the rich galleon.
He strides the upper deck
under the Spanish flag,
scans the harbor
for the rowboats and crew
overdue at the bells
the riggings undone
an anchor to raise
while the weather encroaches.
My spyglass is blind,
in banks of mist,
there is easy prey

(continued)

Karen E. Wagner
Ashland, MA

set low in the water
in a ship heavy with
doubloons and ornaments,
booty for a cavalier's ransom,
and still I bide my time
until
I can count my fingers,
count my gold.

***

A. McKinne Stires
Westport Island, ME

It's Never Easy

It's never easy
scraping the charred supper
from the pot,
or imagining
what it might have been
if I hadn't tried to write
just a few more lines
while it cooked.
If it's a backward look
at what might have been,
it's never easy mending
the shirt
or the dish
or the heart.

Charles L. Looney
Lihue, HI

Sonnet 4

You said you'd diagram it once for me,
the way our life together would unfold:
the kids, the stomach aches, a messy tea
party in the sofa, roof with a hole
for love to pour through, always love, like rain
to keep us green as grass I wouldn't mow
until we lost the dogs and plastic crane,
until the leaf piles topped the mounds of snow.
But you wouldn't tell me about the end:
was I a failure or a fraud? a drunk
whose bottles drove you finally round the bend?
an accident of ice, road, oaken trunk?
No, I would not see you out of life,
bundled in sheets and tubes, a cancer wife.

***

Donna Bruno
Ft. Lauderdale, FL

Sleep

Sleep
      precious, unattainable
Dream-rest
The balm to which "The Bard" referred
      that "knits up the raveled sleeve of care"
eludes me once again
Ambien, Sominex,
      ineffective—all for naught
There is no "off" switch for my mind
Morning comes too soon

Janet Morgan
Litchfield, ME

Christmas Skates

I had graduated. I could now go where the big kids skated. The Reid family shared their pond with the townspeople, and for that distinction, the town plowed it and put up a three-sided shelter for skaters to sit and put on their skates or rest when tired. But what led up to my first outing to skate a mile from home?

On the Christmas when I was eleven and my cousin Deanna twelve, we were allowed to go to Reid's Pond without adult supervision. I did not know this, however, when I got up early that morning. My father, a shift worker at the local power plant, only got Christmas day off once every four years; he worked the day shift on this holiday. Sometimes my brother Eddie and I were able to convince our parents to open our presents before Dad went to work, but not this year. He would only let us open one gift each before he left. He usually picked out the gift, but this time my mother insisted on selecting my present.

Once my chosen gift was sitting in front of me, I looked up with uncertainty. It surprised me that my father let Mom pass me a fairly large box to open on that pre-dawn morning. He *always* chose a small package, something on the order of a coloring book or crayons, but not both.

As I began to open the box with a red ribbon and bow on top, I could tell it was footwear. Dea and I always snitched and told each other what we were getting on the rare occasions that our mothers let us in on what the other was getting. I knew Dea had new ice skates under her tree, but I never dreamed I would also receive a pair. I had outgrown mine—the old ones cramped my toes—but new ones for me? I doubted it. When I told Dea that she would be getting new skates, she told me I would be too. I didn't believe her. I later learned that she'd had no idea what my big gift would be. She

Janet Morgan
Litchfield, ME

had just been trying to make me feel good.

On that day I ripped at the package, trying to get it open fast to ease the suspense. If it turned out to be boots, I would just die. I *needed*, I *wanted* new ice skates. Breathless with excitement, I pulled back the inner wrapping. And there they were: white figure skates stared back at me. So okay, they looked just like the last pair, but they were my dream come true. After Dad had gone to work, I danced around the room. I asked Mom if I could call Dea. Maybe she would go down back with me so I could use them at the stream.

Mom laughed and said yes. I dashed for the telephone. Dea squealed with delight when she told me about her new skates and asked me what I got. When I told her, she said that she had known all along, but the squeak she emitted made me realize that she'd had no idea. We laughed together and made plans to go skating. Disappointment overwhelmed me when I heard Dea say, "Mom says I can go Reid's Pond today. She's even letting me walk there, if I can get someone to go with me." My heart sank. My mother would never let me walk all the way down there, even though it was my fondest dream. I sighed and told Dea that I would be down back if she wanted to join me.

My dreams dashed, I placed the phone's receiver back onto the cradle. I thought about Dea walking past our house with an older friend or her brother Gary. They would be going to the big pond while I plodded along at the stream. I tried to look happy when I went into the kitchen, where Mom was baking pies for dinner. She hadn't opened any presents. I knew I shouldn't feel sorry for myself, especially when I looked over at my six-year-old brother Eddie sitting at the kitchen table with his new coloring book and old, broken crayons, happy and oblivious.

"What did Dea say about skating with you today?" my mother asked.

"Oh, she's going to Reid's Pond. I guess I'll go down back." I was just thinking about inviting Eddie to join me in

Janet Morgan
Litchfield, ME

his boots—for he did not have skates yet but he did like to pretend—when I heard the most marvelous words in the world.

"You didn't want to go to Reid's Pond with Dea?"

"*Me*?" My voice squeaked. "But I can't go there. You said so last year."

"Oh, but this is another year. You're older now. If you want to go, I can drive you and Dea down. You *will* have to walk home, though."

I dashed for the phone on feet that tripped with happiness. Dea let out a war whoop that nearly split my ear when I told her the good news. Gary had other plans, so Dea jumped at my mother's invitation. It wasn't long before we were being driven to the pond where all the townie teenagers congregated. Cool! Mom let us out and drove off with Eddie looking back at us through the side window. I had a twinge of guilt for him, but realized that he wouldn't be able to walk a whole mile back home when we finished skating.

I forgot all about Eddie, however, as Dea and I entered the shelter, sat on a bench and donned our skates before we gracefully glided across the ice. Well, not really. We fell down bunches of times and had sore bottoms before we decided we'd had enough. Deliriously happy, we took off our skates, tied the long laces together in a bow and slung them over our necks. The skates bumped against our small chests while we walked. We talked about all the fun we'd had: falling, tripping and picking ourselves up again. We laughed and laughed. It was the best day of my young life.

We were halfway home when we were offered a ride. Having walked on frozen stumps during the first half of the journey, I was ready to dive into the back seat as the driver stepped out of her car and opened the back driver's-side door. Then I heard Dea issue those dreaded words: "No, thank you. My mother said to never accept rides from strangers."

She isn't a stranger, I wanted to cry out, but I was too

Janet Morgan
Litchfield, ME

stunned to speak. This was a neighbor, *and* a close friend of our grandmother. She wasn't going to kidnap us! What could Dea be thinking? The elderly lady just nodded and sped off. "Dea," I protested, "my feet are cold and Mrs. Metcalf is Gram's friend. She isn't a stranger."

"Yeah, but Mom said she's a horrible driver and to never take a ride from her."

Upset, I barely spoke to Dea all the way home. It was years later—when I saw Mrs. Metcalf park her car in a ditch at a 45-degree angle at a yard sale—that I finally saw the wisdom of Dea's words.

***

Patrick T. Randolph
Lincoln, NE

Home for a Holiday Visit

My father sits across from me,
Holding onto his wrinkled hands
Like a cherished baseball never to be
Let go of—He looks down at his large
Fingers, moves them around to keep them
Warm on this frigid December morning.

"You were so small—my new son," he says.
"I looked at you through that frozen nursery
Window. It was cold outside—an icy Wisconsin
Morning. I often think of you on that day. What magic."

I listen to his gentle voice. We embrace each other,
Dismissing the space between us. The concept, the words,
The sound of "I love you," becomes too small for this
      moment.

Steve Troyanovich
Florence, NJ

soaring eagle blues

for Jim Pepper

a requiem of stillness
fills the aching notes
of a solitary snowman's cry...

crevices whispering memories
flicker into the sounds
of a flying eagle's final song...

can you hear my shadow?
can you touch my heart?
it is calling you...
a gaunt wind tumults
hosting ghosts

between these cold shapes
and the moon's bent bow
lonely wings
usher the primal dream
swelling up from the earth...

darkness is the eye of the star's lost ember
darkness is a blanket of once and forever...
darkness is the cradle
of a saxophone's wail

Cindy Partington
Dallas Center, IA

The Send-Off

full freight cars waited
while the human cargo
funneled up narrow stairs
her father
hovered near the engine
in the gathering steam clouds
of building pressure
he raised calloused hands
to just above the black surface
and sprinkled holy water
from a tiny vial
sending a spray of evaporating
hisses skyward
with his prayers
his whispered blessing lost
in the babble and din
he wondered
who would bless the ship

the leavers
watched the baggage car
swallow their trunks whole
then hand in unwrinkled hand
hurried along the worn planks
toward goodbyes

her mother's arms
surrounded each of them in turn
patting their backs
her voice managed
to calmly wish them a safe journey
a good life

Cindy Partington
Dallas Center, IA

then her shaking hands
gave her daughter a softly wrapped trove
of embroidered baby clothes
saying
"So my hands may
touch my grandchildren."

***

Diane H. Schetky
Topsham, ME

Ode to Garlic

A
garlic
bulb is a
thing of beauty
shaped like the old onion
domes of Russian Orthodox
Churches, designed to help prayers
find their way to Heaven

Beneath
garlic's papery skin
smooth shapely haunches
cradle the smaller cloves within.
Cooked or raw, it is hard to resist garlic's allure.
It is sought out by suitors for soups, sauces, sausages
olive oil, mussels, pasta and pesto and escargots.
Their marriages endure and
find their way to culinary Heaven.

A. McKinne Stires
Westport Island, ME

Caretaker's Lament

The ancient house, once filled with steamy whispers
from stews on the wood stove,
has been reduced to a cellar hole,
filled with the rubble of a dream,
a crater crowned with sumacs and lilacs
standing vigil in a mist of memories.

The last caretaker had screwed his existence to
conserving the dream of the builder.
He was the last to hear its floors creak,
the last to patch the leaking roof,
the last to feel the warmth of its hearth
after the others had gone,
the last to feel the pull of the mission,
clinging to his bones.

He felt it suck, like a leech, and still he dreamed
that his grandchildren, and their children,
would run through the rooms of the house.
While he was young, hope rose with him like a sun,
and let him sleep at night, but
in his waning years, as he thought
of the inevitability of cellar holes,
hope left his body like a spinster's sigh.

He knew his bent, gnarled hands, hardened
from years of stemming the tide of decay,
some day would lie, limp as rope,
at the sides of his ashen body at rest,
in an earthen hole of its own.

Jim Talbot
Rockport, ME

Mea Culpa

Scandals, large and small—nascent and mature, often divide people into three groups. First, there's the inner circle, the people actually doing the scandal—they're the most culpable. But there's almost always a second group that knows about the activities of the first group and yet does nothing to stop them—they also bear some responsibility. Finally, there's the public at large who react with righteous indignation when the scandal is exposed. However, their sanctimonious cries often mask the anguish of those caught up in the scandal through nothing more than force of circumstance.

When I graduated from college on Saturday, June 4th, 1966, the Vietnam War had already been raging for several years. But it seemed to reach a kind of critical mass about the time I was marching to "Pomp and Circumstance" to receive my Bachelor of Science in Chemical Engineering. With so many of my contemporaries marching to military music, in close-order formation, while carrying an M-14 or M-16 rifle, I had hedged my future by applying for Air Force officer training during the winter of my senior year.

In the spring of that year, I accepted a position at a *major oil corporation* chemical plant in Calumet City, Illinois, a few miles southeast of Chicago near the Indiana border. They manufactured two products, concentrated formaldehyde and polyethylene emulsions, but also served as a distribution center for other company products. While the company was flexible as to when I started, I wanted to report as early as possible so I could start earning the big salary I had been promised.

The fly in my ointment was the letter I had received from my Uncle Sam just before the end of my last semester. It said, in clear neglect of my plans, I was ordered to report (in

Jim Talbot
Rockport, ME

my hometown about 500 miles away) for a Selective Service draft physical at 0600 on Monday, June 6th—a mere thirty-six hours after receiving my diploma, returning my cap and gown, and departing school for the last time. I was looking forward to realizing the financial reward for five years of hard study and work, and had bought, on-time, a mint green, 1965 Pontiac GTO with bucket seats, four-on-the-floor, tachometer, and a 389 cubic inch Tri Power engine with a big phony air scoop on the hood. I was proud of that car, but with these two competing reporting requirements, I was a little uncertain, and apprehensive, about just where my life was headed.

Fortunately, the two competing forces demanding my presence soon reached an accommodation with each other. Shortly after the physical, my draft board declared me 1A, "Fit for military service and available to be drafted," which at that time meant I would be drafted very soon. But then, after filing an appeal, with a written endorsement by my plant manager, and making a personal appearance before the draft board, I was reclassified as 1S, "Deferred because of the needs of a critical occupation." Concentrated formaldehyde (in short supply nationally and being ordered on a priority basis by the federal government) is needed in the manufacture of explosives used in bombs and artillery shells. Now I was free to pursue a life of affluence and pleasure, uninterrupted by the Vietnam War.

As I settled-in to my new *major oil corporation* job, I soon learned one of my daily tasks was to start a rented, gasoline-powered, portable pump with one and half inch fire hoses, to dispose of some of our industrial waste into the Little Calumet River. (The river was about six hundred feet wide at this point, formed one boundary of the plant property, and emptied into Lake Michigan in about eight miles.) This was needed to keep our off-spec polyethylene emulsion waste, a milk-like liquid contained in open, dirty sludge ponds, from inundating the plant. I was to start the pump at dusk and

Jim Talbot
Rockport, ME

then turn it off about two hours before first light so the white plume in the river could mix and blend with the offensive water already fouled by other up-stream companies.

The on/off timing of the pump operation was critical because the State of Illinois had initiated law enforcement water patrols of the river to ensure compliance with the fledgling environmental laws being enacted by governing legislatures (the Federal Clean Water law wouldn't become effective until 1974). Since further polluting of the river was not only unethical but now probably illegal, the company management had decided we couldn't ask any unionized hourly employees to perform this task and the job would have to be done by whichever salaried supervisor was on duty, i.e., me when I rotated onto the evening and midnight shifts. In addition, I was cautioned not to talk to any of the hourly workers about what we were doing.

I was twenty-two years old, taking the first step in my professional career, but I was already savvy enough to see a rock when I looked to my right and a hard place when I looked to my left. There was no dodging responsibility, I was an inner circle doer, not some innocent observer—it was my hand on the throttle. But, if I objected to this task and was fired, resigned in protest, or tried to change jobs, I'd not only leave without a good job recommendation, but my draft status would immediately revert to 1A. So despite a deepening angst gnawing at my psyche, I continued to pump the unsightly, but non-toxic, industrial waste into the Little Calumet River.

But then one day in early October I received a letter from my other Uncle Sam. It said, that if I'd only quit my job and enlist in the United States Air force, I'd be entered into a twelve week training program, and if I successfully completed that program, I'd be commissioned as a Second Lieutenant. Interestingly, I was physically disqualified from being an Army or Navy Officer, but not from the Air Force's Officer Corps. After some deliberation, I accepted their offer.

Jim Talbot
Rockport, ME

Major life decisions often have a way of sneaking up on you so that you don't quite realize their significance until long after you've made them.

Because, I was slotted to be a computer maintenance officer, the Air Force assigned me to a ten-month electronics school at Keesler Air Force Base in Biloxi, MS; because, I was sitting in the officers club, feeling somewhat sorry for myself, on Friday night, 10 February, 1967, I met—quite by accident—one of Mississippi's most charming and attractive young ladies; because, I fell in love with this woman, I married her and together we raised two of the most wonderful children any parents could hope for; and because, my life—including a twenty-two year military career with overseas tours at an air base in Thailand during the Vietnam War and at a NATO headquarters in Italy during the Cold War—filled me with many poignant memories I want to preserve for my descendants in a family history, I wrote this paper.

As to the *major oil corporation* plant, I've good reason to believe what we were doing was not unknown to at least some local authorities. But over time, the political dynamic changed. To this day, I don't know if management decided on their own they would have to absorb the extra cost of a more environmentally friendly waste disposal protocol, whether they were gently nudged in that direction by some governmental "cease and desist order," or whether a full-fledged scandal evolved with a raid by law enforcement officers carrying side arms and search warrants leading to criminal indictments, fines and/or jail time. But when I returned for a visit a few years later the property was owned by a different company and I couldn't see the sludge ponds.

When I look at Google Earth satellite photos of the plant area, I can still see the Little Calumet River, the location of the sludge ponds, and some of the buildings that were there in 1966. During my lifetime, I've seen many scandals play-out in the media, but of all these, the scandal that changed my life the most, was the one I chose to run from.

Roselyn Stewart
Brookfield, WI

Sojourners

I've set the table
for breakfast
Coffee mugs,
medications

We arise,
unsteadily
lurch forward
our dreams
forgotten

Silver streaks our
hair as we struggle
through daily tasks
The wolf grows bolder

Weeks repeat
faster and faster
as though we ride
a carrousel
gone awry

Yet life is
beautiful
We have good times
and each other

Anne Cyr
Buxton, ME

My Ears, Your Eyes

We've always been a feisty pair—
more ruffled feathers than mutual preening,
often jostling for dominance
like birds at the feeder,
as obstinate as oak leaves spinning in the breeze
still attached to the tree
while snowflakes fall in mid March.

These last weeks of winter,
while my husband recovers
from yet another knee surgery,
I've enjoyed my solitary walks.
I trot along snowmobile trails,
through woods and fields
and by the river—even *on* the river,
if I'm feeling brave enough.
Occasionally I sink through the snow
to my knees, but upon gaining footing
chant "Up, up, up," to myself
as if by doing so I become lighter.

Today we walked together
for the first time in weeks,
up and down the length of our road.
He set a brisk pace—
a remarkable recovery.
At the top I declare a halt:
I could hear a cardinal cheering away,
a rare event in our neck of the woods.
Then a titmouse joined in with his clear
pee-er, pee-er, pee-er.

(continued)

Anne Cyr
Buxton, ME

We linger awhile listening to their duet,
these two birds just loud enough
for my husband's impaired hearing.
He stood with his head tilted,
a broad smile across his face.

"Time to slow down," he announced
as we turn around and head to the other end.
He gestures to the raw looking cavities
a woodpecker had recently drilled,
riddling the side of a distressed pine.
Wood chips are mounded at its base,
amber-hued against the snow.
He points out how you can see
small tunnels within the holes;
signs of woodboring beetles—
the meal the bird was seeking—
a detail I would never have noticed
walking on my own.

When we reach the farm
whose fields roll down to the river,
I stop us once again as I detect a thin,
high-pitched chorus of birds.
"Listen—can you hear it?"
He shakes his head no—too far out of his range.
"Where's it coming from?" he asks.
I nod to the tall trees
in the yard out in front of us
and just like that he says,
"There they are."

And what I had thought were stubborn leaves
clinging to the top of the tree
suddenly take off in a burst of flight,

(continued)

Anne Cyr
Buxton, ME

heading for the woods, singing as they go.
"Must be cedar waxwings," he declares.
I twirl around to follow the birds' flight,
then dance over to take his arm
and pull him close.

***

P. C. Moorehead
North Lake, WI

Do You Know?

Do you know
what it means
to be seen,
to be really seen,
to be heard,
to be heard
with the perfect pitch
of one who has heard the same song
and sung it?

Do you know what it means?

Juliana L'Heureux
Topsham, ME

Les Frères: Among America's Greatest Generation

Connaître les affres de la guerre

Among the young men from Maine who fought in World War II were five L'Heureux brothers, Franco-Americans from Sanford (one died prior to being interviewed). Their memories were vivid and startling, as though they had never left the scenes they described.

America's greatest generation includes this once silent group of five heroes. Their numbers dwindled, even since they met for this interview. Only Robert is still alive, living in Sanford. For many World War II veterans, reliving their experiences during those horrible war years has been difficult and, understandably, emotional.

They were courageous soldiers who served during an era we know through movies, where their bravery was portrayed by larger than life actors who tried to reenact their battlefield horror. Although humble, they were obviously the heroes of their generation, during a time defined by The Great Depression that was sandwiched between two 20th century world wars.

Young people today are challenged to answer questions about what college they plan to attend or where to work after high school, in the 1940s, the big questions were pointedly about survival and sacrifice.

"What is your draft number?" was in the uppermost minds of 18 and 19-year-olds during the distressing years 1940–45, during World War II.

Like in many Sanford families, the five L'Heureux brothers made their mother and father, Blanche and Albert, "Silver Star" parents. It was distinction they surely did not seek, but was recognition of their supreme sacrifice. As part of the Silver Star program, the parents were involved in

Juliana L'Heureux
Topsham, ME

efforts on the home front where they could support bringing their children safely home.

Fate may have intervened in their survival, but they hold their return home to the power of plenty of prayers. In fact, all five brothers returned home alive, although two were wounded.

Robert ("Bob" now 93—living in Sanford), along with his brothers—all of them now deceased since the taped interview—Walter, Henry and Arthur agreed to meet and talk about their rarely shared war memories of military service and fighting on the Pacific and European fronts. For Henry, especially, the war was still vivid. "Even my three bothers have never heard some of this before now. Believe me! I saw even more than I've talked about," he said.

Henry's difficult to discuss descriptions about personal survival in the face of horribly close combat with the German Nazis in Europe provide a miraculous example about the emotional power of prayer. In his case, the prayers of his mother and family sustained him through unbelievable ordeals.

Henry and Bob received Purple Hearts, when they were wounded in Europe. Arthur and Walter fought in the Pacific, in the Philippines, Australia and in Japan.

As teenagers, they were drafted to fight. The brothers sadly recalled how their father, Albert, walked them from their home in Sanford to the bus stop located near the corner of Main and Washington Streets, when it was their time to leave.

Although each young man left for the service at a different time, all five brothers were gone between 1941—1945.

Robert is somber when he recalls how sad his father looked as the bus slowly pulled out of Sanford after the two said good-bye. It's a memory the four men find difficult to talk about, even after the passage of more than 50 years. "Don't forget to write," is what Albert said to his son during their good-bye.

Juliana L'Heureux
Topsham, ME

"I could see his tears," said Robert. "But, I wondered, could my father see mine?"

Years later, Robert learned how his father spoke with someone at the bus stop about his feelings. "I just gave another boy to the army," his father told an observer on that day of separation.

Daily prayers and the devout faith of their Franco-American parents, Albert and Blanche, sustained the family during the difficult war years. They were joyously rewarded when the family was able to enjoy a reunion after the war. In fact, Albert was so happy to see his five sons home and safely together, he even broke the family's rule against allowing them to drink at home. For the first time, their father let them drink beer while they rejoiced on the family's front porch.

"We prayed every day to the Blessed Virgin," recalled Henry about his heroic attempts to fight for his life when the odds seemed dead set against him surviving. But, nearly miraculously, he survived a series of bloody and brutal battles.

In fact, the 1944 U.S. invasion of Anzio beachhead in Italy (January 22–May 29, 1944) brought Henry to his first miraculously survived incident. His mother's life saving prayers may have arrived in the form of a package. Henry, as a first gunner, said he was "penned down" in the same area for three months when a package was delivered to him and a fellow soldier who were stationed at their machine gun. "LAAarooooo!" yelled the delivery man who dropped the package into his gunner site. "This is from home!"

Soon, both Henry and his comrade found themselves acutely ill with stomach cramps from devouring the cookies in the package, which had spoiled in transit. So, they left their machine gun post to vomit in a nearby stream. In an instant, while the two were at the stream, their gun post was directly hit with enemy fire and completely blown up. They had escaped certain death thanks to the miracle of those

Juliana L'Heureux
Topsham, ME

spoiled cookies. "My mother's love saved my life," said Henry.

Of course, enormous media attention is given to the Allied invasion of Normandy, France under troops commanded by General Dwight D. Eisenhower that gets the attention of modern movies and books. But, as Henry witnessed, an equally horrible picture of death and devastation awaited Allied troops in 1944, in Anzio, Italy.

"The guys were blown up all around me on Anzio beachhead. Twice, I was the only survivor. When I looked around, I was the only one left. Blood was flying around like rain. The blood fell on me like rain," Henry recalled, while crying. "I was all alone, all alone. All my friends were dead."

Henry was also with the Third Infantry Division when they fought during the bloody battle for Monte Cassino.

After seeing the horrendous carnage at Anzio, Henry didn't make friends with his comrades anymore, because he never knew when they would be killed in combat. "I only knew them a few days," he said. (Henry's emotional interview is audio taped.)

On May 24, 1944, about five miles south of Rome, Henry earned his Purple Heart. "Fighting on the way to Rome was hell. We slept maybe one hour at a time. Every day was like hell. Then I was wounded," he said.

Even his wound was a spiritual experience. Henry says he prayed every night about being wounded. "In my prayer, I asked to get wounded in my little finger so it would never show. In fact, his prayer was answered when a bullet hit his little finger, just as he had prayed. His one regret was the injury prevented him from moving with his unit into Rome, where he wanted to see the Vatican. He never got to Rome.

Although Henry's wound temporarily took him out of combat, it didn't keep him away from the front lines of the war for very long. Soon, he was back in the European war where he continued to see combat and even more unimaginable horror, first hand.

Juliana L'Heureux
Topsham, ME

"Did you kill Nazis," I asked him?

"Yes, I killed some....No, I killed more than some," Henry said, in what was a profoundly difficult moment. A moment of silence followed.

Among Henry's modest collection of war memorabilia is a small Nazi insignia he cut from the uniform of the very first man he had shot and killed. "I prayed for him," he explains. "I prayed for him when I cut off this emblem."

While Henry fought in repeated engagements in Southern Europe, his brother Bob was involved in the June 1944 Allied invasion of Normandy. Bob was a Private First Class (PFC), working with communications when he landed nine days after the first bloody Allied invasion of France.

"Operation Overlord" was the code name for the Invasion of Normandy on the French coast and the establishment of Allied forces in France in 1944, during World War II. It was the largest amphibious operation to ever take place.

Allied land forces in combat during the Normandy invasion on June 6th, came from Canada, the Free French Forces, the United Kingdom and the United States. In weeks following the invasion, Polish forces also participated with the Royal Australian Air Force and Royal Norwegian Navy. http://en.wikipedia.org/wiki/Invasion_of_Normandy.

Bob recalls how he arrived in a ship. "We got off on a pontoon bridge. We landed at four o'clock and I saw some brown things on the beach. I asked what those brown things were and was told they were GI bodies."

While in Normandy, Bob was able to call on his Franco-American heritage to bridge a language friendship with local people. He was able to communicate with a seven-year-old boy named Gigi Letourneau, who quickly learned how to get American chocolate bars from the funny soldier who could even speak to him in French. Bob called the boy "Gee."

"Viens ici (Come here)," Bob asked the boy. "We were dug in about 200 yards from him when I gave the kid chocolate. He told me it was the first time he ever ate chocolate."

Juliana L'Heureux
Topsham, ME

Eventually, the boy asked Bob to meet his mother. To Bob's surprise, the boy's mother was the same age as his own mother, Blanch, in Sanford. "I went to their house at night. Gee's mother liked to hear me talk French so much," he says. Mrs. Letourneau wrote letters to Blanch in French. Several months later, on November 29, 1944, Bob was wounded near the Rhine River in Germany and he also received a Purple Heart.

Many years later, Bob and his wife Theresa visited Normandy where they searched for and eventually found the man who was the young boy "Gigi," who he befriended with chocolate.

Unfortunately, Mrs. Letourneau had died about one month before Bob and Theresa's visit.

While visiting Normandy as a World War II veteran, Bob admired a handmade wooden crucifix hanging in a Catholic Church near the village where the Letourneau's lived. He looked to buy one just like it as a memory of his experiences in Normandy. Instead, Theresa suggested he carve one for himself. So, when they returned home to Sanford, he did just that.

On the Pacific front, Walter and his brother Arthur experienced war in other horrible ways, but just as nightmarish as their two siblings who were in Europe. Rather than the often close and even hand-to-hand combat of Europe, they saw other horrors. One effect was the results of torture inflicted on Filipino women in Manila by Japanese, who forcibly compelled them into prostitution.

Arthur said he often unexpectedly saw decaying and unclaimed bodies of Japanese while walking around the streets of Manila in the Philippines during the US occupation. He witnessed body parts floating in the water or the carcasses of people shot to death on abandoned train cars. He could only imagine what happed, how they were killed and left behind.

Walter and Arthur experienced a very special surprise

Juliana L'Heureux
Topsham, ME

moment in Manila when they enjoyed an unexpected meeting at a USO entertainment show. Walter was promoted to first sergeant within nine months of being drafted. He eventually wound up working in engineering unit unloading heavy equipment in Manila. Arthur was also a sergeant serving with the occupation army in Manila. Walter saw that his brother's outfit number and company was in Manila, so he went to the USO show to try to find him.

Someone got a message to Sergeant Arthur L'Heureux about someone wanting to see him. It was startling for Arthur when he saw his brother Walter was waiting to greet him. His unexpected reunion helped Arthur's loneliness, a little, while he was serving in Manila amid the war carnage.

"We were not always good boys, but we sure prayed a lot," said Arthur.

Walter found his passion to play baseball helped pass time when he wasn't working with heavy equipment. He was noticed for being an excellent baseball pitcher. (In fact, Walter is a member of Maine's Baseball Hall of Fame.) In perhaps the biggest game of his life, he pitched to baseball's great icon Joe DiMaggio and to his brother Don, when he played opposite them both at a U.S. Army baseball tournament, in Australia. Amazingly, Walter struck out Don DiMaggio when he pitched five scoreless innings against the DiMaggio brothers on the opposing team. Unfortunately, Walter's team lost the game, but the stats put Walter into Maine's B84
aseball Hall of Fame. Walter is among Maine's baseball heroes listed along with President George H.W. Bush, who played collegiate baseball in York County leagues, when he was home in Kennebunkport, during his Yale college years.

Interviewing the L'Heureux brothers even 50 years after their World War II experiences was personal evidence about how war memories don't fade away with time. Their recollections were just as vivid as though they had recently happened. Their memories were the true life experiences now

Juliana L'Heureux
Topsham, ME

being archived by many historical societies and in family memoirs.

Henry's war experiences continued beyond his combat. Tragically, he was eyewitness to the human ashes found in wine casks during the liberation of Holocaust death camps, where thousands of Jews were tortured and cremated.

"No one can tell me the killing of Jews did not happen." His anger blew at some modern attempts to redefine the murders of six million Jews. He has nothing but disdain for the Holocaust denial by people who don't acknowledge the murder of innocent Jews, in addition to other designated ethnic groups, by Nazis during World War II. These mass murders were part of the heinous genocide Hitler ordered in his horror scheme to create one white master human race. Hitler compounded the junk science of eugenics with racism as the basis for the extermination of millions of people.

Before his death, Henry worked with Veteran's Administration supporters who were interested in sponsoring more recognition for his personal and extraordinary dedication and bravery during World War II.

It took three hours to interview the four surviving L'Heureux brothers about their extraordinary Word War II experiences. Thankfully, some of their discussion is captured on audiotape. Their stories complement a long and proud family history of military service. Moreover, their ability to relate their personal stories is a touching confirmation about the brothers' bravery and their faithful camaraderie in the face of very difficult and, at times, wrenchingly emotional recollections.

Let's hope Americans continue to appreciate the importance of Veterans Day for what our heroes of all wars have given to protect our nation's freedom from tyranny. Otherwise, as the cliché warns, "Those who forget history are doomed to repeat it."

Ceux qui oublient l'histoire sont condamnés à le répéter.

Juliana L'Heureux
Topsham, ME

On November 11, 1995, the US World War II Veterans Memorial in Washington DC was finally dedicated to The Greatest Generation.

***

Robert B. Moreland
Pleasant Prairie, WI

Normandy

The flag now waves above the field,
white stones set out in rows arrayed.
Countless sons lie whose fate now sealed,
died then our freedom be displayed.

Waves crash among the parapets,
medal posthumous honor gets.
Forget-me-nots among the green,
my heart stopped here; GI, eighteen.

Original citation: Moreland, R.B. "Normandy" in Moreland, R.B. and Miner, K.M. Postcards from *Baghdad: Honoring America's Heroes*. Xlibris (Philadelphia, PA, 2008) p81.

GOOSE RIVER ANTHOLOGY, 2017

We seek selections of fine poetry, essays, and short stories (3,000 words or less) for the 15th annual *Goose River Anthology, 2017*. The book will be beautifully produced with full color cover and full color dust jacket for hard covers.

You may submit even if you have been published before in a previous edition of the *Goose River Anthology*. We retain one-time publishing rights. All rights revert back to the author after publication. You may submit as many pieces as you like.

EARN CASH ROYALTIES. Author will receive a 10% royalty on all sales that he or she generates.

There is no purchase required and nothing is required of the author for publication. Deadline for submissions is April 30, 2017. Publication will be in the fall of 2017 (they make great Christmas gifts). Guidelines are as follows:

- Submit clean, typed copy by snail mail—**mandatory**
- Email a Word or rtf file to us (if possible)
- Reading fee: $1.00 per page
- Do not put two poems on the same page
- Essays and short stories must be double-spaced
- **SASE for notification** (one forever stamp) plus additional postage for possible return of submission if desired.
- Author's name & address at top of each page of paper copy and first page of emailed copies.

Submit to:
Goose River Anthology, 2017
3400 Friendship Road
Waldoboro, ME 04572-6337
E mail: gooseriverpress@roadrunner.com
www.gooseriverpress.com